J916.81 9890
Car
Carpenter, Allan, Balow, Tom

Enchantment of Africa Botswana.

DATE DUE

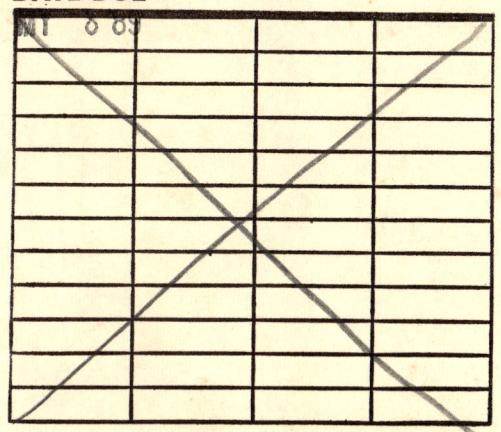

Guthrie Center Public Library
Guthrie Center, Iowa
RULES

Children and adults are entitled to draw books upon filling out application blank.

Each borrower is responsible for all books drawn on his card, and must pay for any book lost or injured.

All books, except 7 day books, may be kept two weeks, and may be renewed for another two weeks.

A fine of two cents a day will be imposed on all books kept overtime.

DEMCO

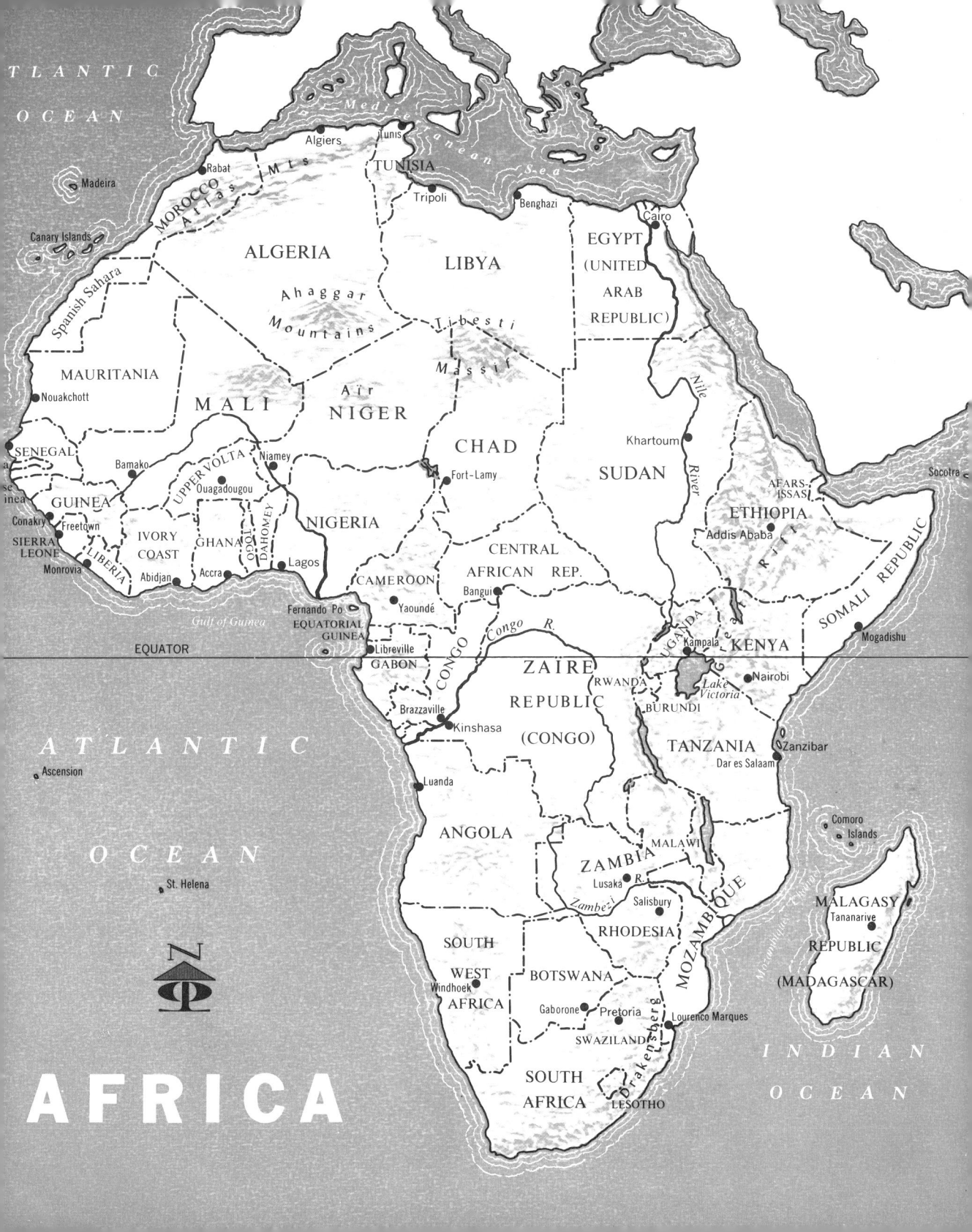

AFRICA

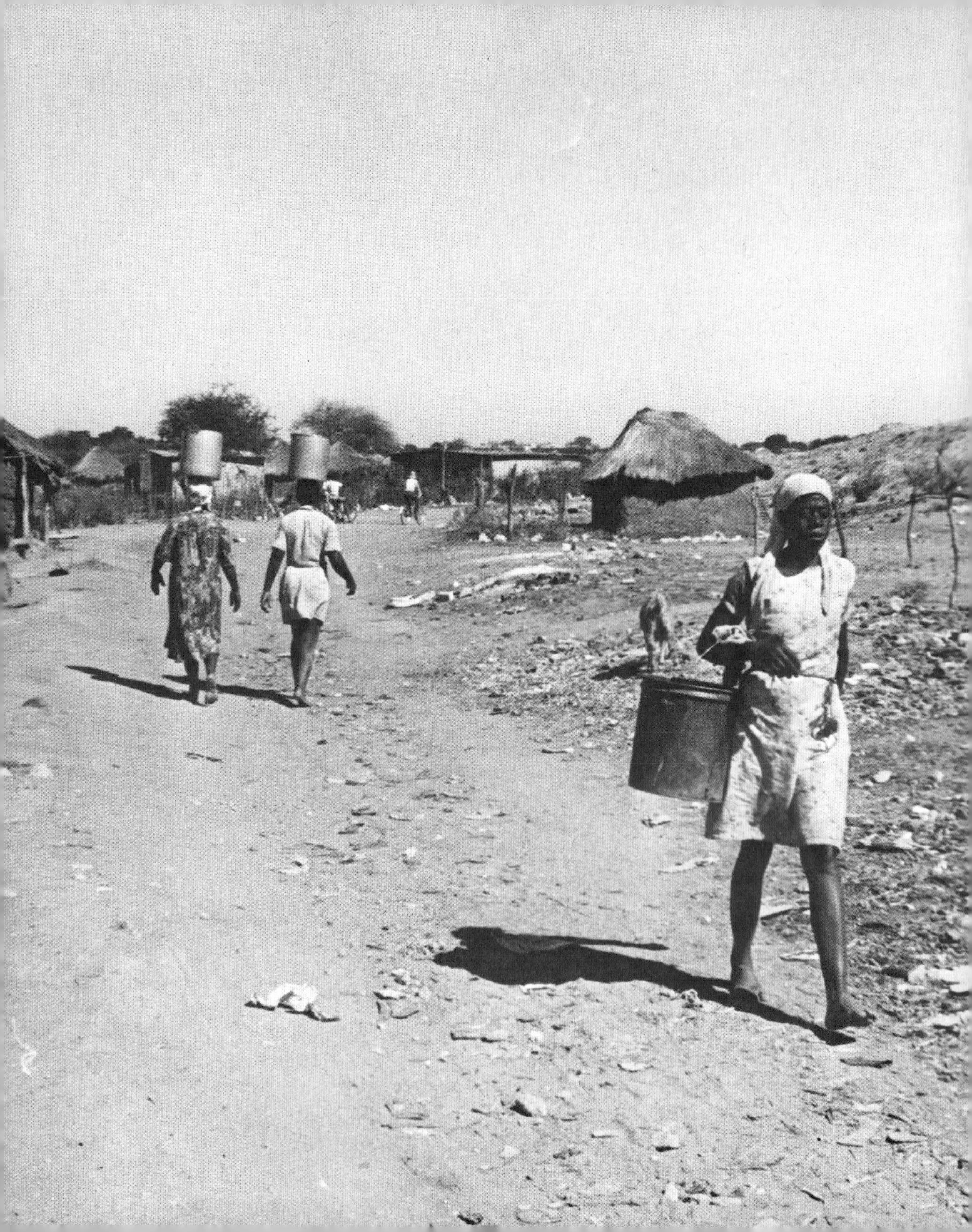

Enchantment of Africa

BOTSWANA

by ALLAN CARPENTER
and TOM BALOW

Consulting Editor
Ronald Cohen, Ph.D.
African Studies Faculty
Northwestern University
Evanston, Illinois

CHILDRENS PRESS, CHICAGO

THE ENCHANTMENT OF AFRICA

Available now: Botswana, Egypt (United Arab Republic), Kenya, Malagasy Republic (Madagascar), Zambia
Planned for the future, six each season: Algeria, Burundi, Cameroon, Central African Republic, Chad, Congo (Brazzaville), Dahomey, Equatorial Guinea, Ethiopia, Gabon, Gambia, Ghana, Guinea, Ivory Coast, Lesotho, Liberia, Libya, Malawi, Mali, Mauritania, Morocco, Niger, Nigeria, Rhodesia, Rwanda, Senegal, Sierra Leone, Somali Republic, South Africa, South West Africa, Sudan, Tanzania, Togo, Tunisia, Uganda, Upper Volta, Zaïre Republic (Congo Kinshasha)

BOARD OF ADVISERS, THE PROGRAM OF AFRICAN STUDIES
NORTHWESTERN UNIVERSITY, EVANSTON, ILLINOIS

GWENDOLEN M. CARTER, Ph.D., Director
Ibrahim Abu-Lughod, Ph.D., Associate Director

Janet Abu-Lughod, Ph.D.
Irma Adelman, Ph.D.
Ethel Albert, Ph.D.
Robert Armstrong, Ph.D.
Jack Beckstrom, L.Lm.
Jack Berry, Ph.D.
P.J. Bohannan, D.Phil.
Dennis Brutus, B.A.
Donald T. Campbell, Ph.D.
Remi Clignet, Doctorat de Recherches
Ronald Cohen, Ph.D.
George Dalton, Ph.D.
Ralph E. Dolkart, M.D.
Johannes Fabian, Ph.D.
Morris Goodman, Ph.D.
Ted R. Gurr, Ph.D.
Errol Harris, D.Litt.
Peter J. Jacobi, M.S.J.
James Johnson, M.A.
Robert Koester, M.S.
Omalara Leslie, B.A.
Sidney J. Levy, Ph.D.

Judith L. McAfee, M.L.S.
S. Sultan Ali Marashi, B.A.
David Michener, M.S.
Johannes Mlela, B.A.
Leon Moses, Ph.D.
Rae Moore Moses, Ph.D.
Alexander Nekam, S.J.D.
John Paden, Ph.D.
Hans E. Panofsky, M.S.
John Rowe, Ph.D.
David Rubadiri, M.A.
Edward W. Soja, Ph.D.
Frank Spalding, J.D.
Richard Spears, Ph.D.
Lindley J. Stiles, Ed.D.
Stuart Streuver, Ph.D.
Klaus Wachsmann, Ph.D.
Douglas Ward, Ed.D.
David Welsh, M.A.
Ralph L. Westfall, Ph.D.
Rodney White, M.S.
E.H. Timothy Whitten, Ph.D.
Ivor Wilks, Ph.D.
Frank Willett, M.A.
Roland Young, Ph.D.

ACKNOWLEDGMENTS

Embassy of Botswana, Washington, D.C.; Charge d'Affaires, Embassy of the U.S., Gaborone, Botswana; Botswana Information Services, Gaborone, Botswana; Saul Motinga, U.S. Information Services, Gaborone, Botswana; M. Tladi, Botswana Information Services, Gaborone, Botswana.

Cover Photograph: Elephant at Chobe Game Reserve, Allan Carpenter
Frontispiece: A village near Francistown, Botswana Information Services

Series Coordinator: Michael Roberts
Project Editor: Joan Downing
Assistant Editor: Janis Fortman
Manuscript Editor: Elizabeth Rhein
Map Artist: Donald G. Bouma

LIBRARY OF CONGRESS
CATALOGING IN PUBLICATION DATA

Carpenter, John Allan, 1917-
  Botswana.
  (Enchantment of Africa)

  SUMMARY: Introduces the land, history, economy, culture, and people of the southern African country much of whose territory includes the Kalahari Desert.
  1. Botswana—Juvenile Literature. [1. Botswana]
I. Balow, Tom, joint author. II. Title.
DT791.C37   916.8'1   72-10379
ISBN 0-516-04553-9

Copyright © 1973, Regensteiner Publishing Enterprises, Inc.
All rights reserved. Printed in the U.S.A.
Published simultaneously in Canada

Contents

A TRUE STORY TO SET THE SCENE 7
   To London, to Visit the Queen

THE FACE OF THE LAND 10
   The Land of Botswana—Swamps and Salt Pans—The Sands of the Kalahari—Climate

THREE CHILDREN OF BOTSWANA 19
   Kenneth of Shushong—Kopano of Francistown—Tira of the Kalahari

BOTSWANA YESTERDAY 27
   Men of Tswana—Dr. Livingstone—Khama the Great—A Unique Colony—Cecil Rhodes—Two Wars—The Power of the Chiefs—A New Look

BOTSWANA TODAY 39
   Love and Mirrage—Exile and Return—New Parties—Call for Independence—A New Constitution—White Resentment—Planning the Election—Victory for Seretse—The Eighteen Months—A New Republic—Path to the Future—The Government of Botswana—Education

NATURAL TREASURES 55
   Living Things—Mineral Resources

THE PEOPLE LIVE IN BOTSWANA 61
   Population—Language and Religion—The Ethnic Groups—The Bushmen—Villages and Land Laws—Health

THE PEOPLE WORK IN BOTSWANA 73
   A Nation of Farmers—The Only Industry—A Dazzling Promise—Wildlife Drawing Card—Transportation and Communication—Employed and Employable—Neighborly Trade

ENCHANTMENT OF BOTSWANA 83
   Along the Railroad—The New Capital—North to the Border—Chobe Game Reserve—Ngamiland and Ghanzi—Kalahari's Lost Ruins

HANDY REFERENCE SECTION 90
   Instant Facts—Population—Holidays—Local Government—Pronunciation Note—You Have a Date with History

INDEX 92

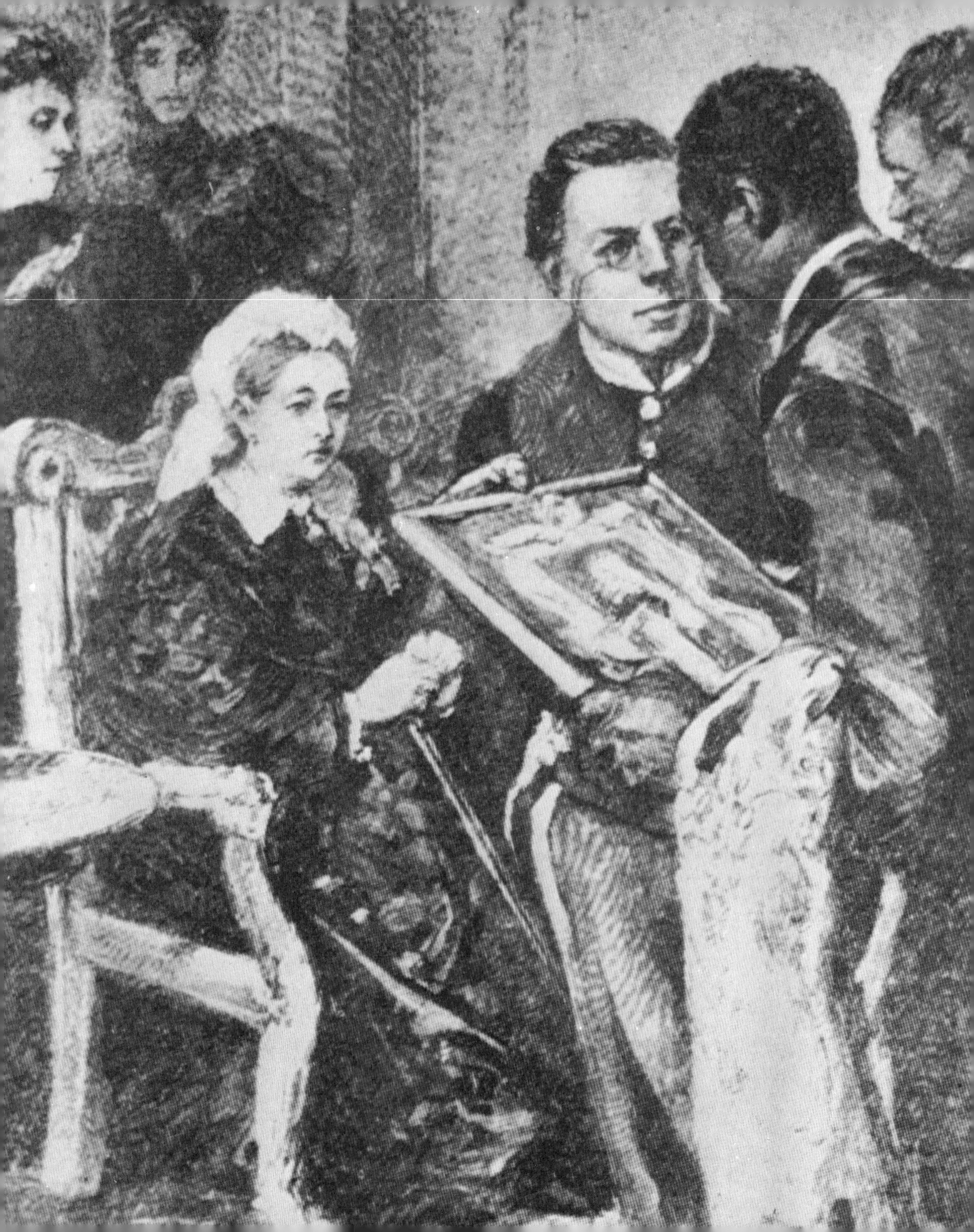

A True Story to Set the Scene

TO LONDON, TO VISIT THE QUEEN

The year is 1895. A short, stout, gray-haired, seventy-six-year-old lady sits on the throne of England. Already she has reigned for fifty-eight years, longer than anyone except George III, her grandfather. In two years she will celebrate her Diamond Jubilee (a celebration that will mark her sixtieth year as queen of England), and her people will demonstrate their admiration and affection for her.

The queen is Victoria. To Great Britain she has brought a time of domestic tranquility. To the rest of the world she has come to represent a dominant force. Her kingdom includes the entire continent of Australia; the subcontinent of India; the sweeping provinces of Canada; possessions in Latin America and the Far East; islands in the Pacific and the West Indies; part of the Antarctic; and colonies that make up about one fourth of the African continent.

Ten years earlier, her government had laid claim to a small, landlocked area in southern Africa. The Bechuanaland Protectorate was not rich in gold or other minerals, nor did it have a large number of British settlers to protect. A road led north from Britain's Cape Colony at the southern tip of Africa through Bechuanaland to the rich mines of what is now Rhodesia. The Dutch Boers from the Transvaal, across the border, were trying to take over Bechuanaland tribal lands for farming purposes. Some of the chiefs asked for the queen's protection and help

Queen Victoria presents her portrait to the Batswana chiefs during their visit in 1895.
MANSELL COLLECTION, RADIO TIMES HULTON PICTURE LIBRARY

The chiefs that visited Queen Victoria are (from left to right) Chief Sebele of the Bakwena, Chief Bathoen of the Bangwaketse, and Chief Khama of the Bamangwato, with Rev. W. C. Willoughby.

MANSELL COLLECTION,
RADIO TIMES HULTON
PICTURE LIBRARY

in fighting the Boers. To protect the people and the road, Victoria became protector of Bechuanaland.

By 1895 the black chiefs of Bechuanaland had become fearful that whites other than the Boers were about to dominate their lands. Victoria had granted a charter for mineral rights in southern Africa to a business organization called the British South Africa Company. Cecil Rhodes, the head of the company, ruled the Cape Colony with a stern hand. He wanted to take control of Bechuanaland so he could build a railroad through it to the mines in the north. Three of Bechuanaland's most powerful chiefs were so outraged at the surrender of the administration of their lands that they decided to complain directly to the queen.

A formal photograph of the three chiefs taken in London during their visit still exists. They are dressed in the heavy, black, thigh-length morning coats and long, gray, flaring trousers fashionable in England at the time. To the left sits Chief Sebele of the Bakwena tribe, a large man with soft, gentle eyes, his legs crossed at the ankles. His father, Chief Sechele, had been converted to Christianity by the missionary David Livingstone, one of the first Englishmen to explore in Bechuanaland.

To Sebele's left sits Chief Khama, one of the greatest African chiefs of the nineteenth century. A tall, thin man with a look of quiet determination, he appears much younger than his sixty-seven years. A Christian convert, he had stopped many of the pagan practices of his tribe, the Bamangwato. He had been the guiding force behind the unification of the peoples of Bechuanaland in keeping the Dutch Boers out and had been the leader in asking for British protection. He is afraid that Rhodes's company will sell his lands to white settlers and that they would allow alcoholic beverages to be sold to his people.

Behind them stands Chief Bathoen of the Bangwaketse tribe, a short, formidable man, his large hand resting on a cane. He had succeeded his father as chief only six years earlier, and he, too, is a Christian. Leaning on a chair next to Chief Bathoen is a small, balding, white man, a London missionary named W. C. Willoughby. He had accompanied the chiefs from their homeland to help with their appeals.

The actual diplomatic conferences with the three chiefs were held by the leaders of Victoria's government, rather than by the queen, as the chiefs had expected. They did have an audience with the queen, however, when she presented each of them with a framed picture of herself and with a formal uniform (of no special rank) to be worn during ritual ceremonies. The aging, white queen who ruled one fourth of the entire world must have been impressed by the noble bearing and the humility of the three black chiefs she had promised to protect.

But queens, and history, can be fickle. As it turned out, the chiefs' long trip to London to visit the queen was not what prevented Cecil Rhodes from taking over Bechuanaland. As a result of the conferences, the British government promised to protect only the chiefs' tribal lands, not all of Bechuanaland. In exchange, the three chiefs agreed to cede narrow strips of land to Rhodes so he could build his railroad.

By using military force against the Boers, Rhodes frightened Queen Victoria into reasserting British control to prevent further hostilities. Early in 1896 the queen issued a proclamation announcing that the Bechuanaland Protectorate would not be administered by the British South Africa Company. This proclamation included the three strips of land Rhodes had briefly controlled.

For the next seventy years the natives of Bechuanaland were to be treated with kindly, though vaguely indifferent, authority by the British colonial government. The Victorian Age was to continue in Bechuanaland long after the death of the queen.

When independence finally came to Bechuanaland in 1966, it came with peace and gentility. It might be said that the new republic called Botswana received its independence in the style of the late Queen Victoria herself.

The Face of the Land

THE LAND OF BOTSWANA

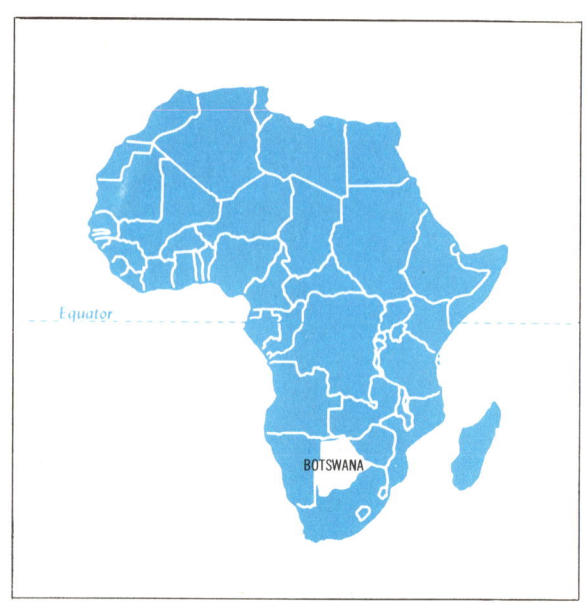

Botswana is a land of contrasts. Much of its surface is covered by the Kalahari Desert; yet it is a land of many rivers. Parts of Botswana average less than an inch of rain a month; yet it has the largest swamp in southern and central Africa. Nothing grows in parts of the hot, dry sands of the Kalahari; yet elsewhere in the country are fertile farmlands and rich grazing areas for cattle. Though Botswana is often beset by lengthy droughts that threaten the lives of both man and beast, sometimes heavy downpours flood the land, similarly threatening its inhabitants.

No one knows exactly how large Botswana is. Figures as high as 275,000 square miles are sometimes given, but most authorities today use a figure of about 220,000 square miles. Botswana is slightly smaller than Texas. Compared to other African territories, it is not especially large; there are twenty larger nations on the continent.

The boundary lines of Botswana are complicated; sometimes they follow rivers and sometimes imaginary lines. To the south and southeast is the Republic of South Africa, the richest and most industrialized country in Africa. This border is formed largely by the Nossob, the Molopo, the Marico, and the Limpopo rivers.

To the west, the border with South West Africa is formed by three straight lines. (South West Africa has been called Namibia by the United Nations since 1968, but that name refers only to its exiled, independent government.) Starting at the southwest, the border follows the line of 20° east longitude, then cuts directly east on the line of 22° south latitude, and continues northward again at 21° east longitude.

The northern border adjoins a narrow band of land called the Caprivi Strip, which separates Botswana from Angola. Part of this border follows the meandering Chobe River. Since 1929 the Caprivi Strip has been part of South West Africa. For a few years before that, it was administered by Botswana.

Rhodesia (called Zimbabwe by black nationalists and liberationists) is Botswana's neighbor to the northeast. The lower part of this border is marked by the Ramaquabane and Shashi rivers.

The border at the extreme northeastern tip of Botswana is sometimes disputed. There is a tiny gap between the Caprivi Strip and Rhodesia where for less than a half-mile—some authorities say only 150 feet—Botswana has a common border with the Republic of Zambia. Here, where the Chobe River meets the Zambezi River, is one of the few spots in the world where four separate nations meet—Botswana, Rhodesia, Zambia, and South West Africa. At this spot missionary-explorer David Livingstone was the first white man to see the Zambezi, the mightiest river in southern Africa. Not far to the east, as the Zambezi flows toward the Indian Ocean, are the great waterfalls Livingstone named for his queen—Victoria Falls.

Like a dozen other countries in Africa, Botswana is landlocked—it does not border an ocean or a sea. It must depend on the friendship of its four bordering neighbors for such things as trade with and travel to the rest of the world.

After gaining independence in 1966, Botswana was divided into twelve councils, or local governing regions. Three of these represent cities; the other nine represent districts, which generally enclose the traditional boundaries of tribal lands.

Before independence, Botswana was known as the Bechuanaland Protectorate and was administered by Great Britain. "Bechuana" (pronounced with a soft "ch") is the way white men first spelled "Batswana," the general name for all the tribes of what is now called "Botswana."

Most of the inhabitants of Botswana live near the southeastern border, where they have been successful in raising cattle and growing some crops. A smaller percentage live to the north, in the swamplands sometimes called Ngamiland. Hardly anyone is able to exist in the arid spread of the Kalahari Desert in the south and central parts of Botswana except for nomadic natives, called Bushmen by outsiders.

SWAMPS AND SALT PANS

In northwestern Botswana is a river, the Okavango, that never reaches a sea. After leaving Angola, the Okavango crosses the Caprivi Strip and runs free and strong through a narrow valley in Botswana for about fifty miles. Then it becomes stopped with weeds, reeds, papyrus, and other growth and begins to meander through uncounted small islands, its waters still clear and clean. This is the mysterious Okavango Swamps, the home of many species of wild animals, birds, fish, and reptiles typical of southern Africa. The swamps cover more than 6,500 square miles, making them the largest swamps in Africa south of the equator.

At the southeastern end of the Okavango Swamps, excess water drains into a river, which in turn drains into two other rivers. These wander through hot, dry lands and sometimes disappear entirely in times of drought. One of these rivers, the Botletle, flows southeast to Lake Xau. The other, the Ngobe, runs southwest to Lake Ngami.

Except in times of flood, when the Okavango brings surplus water, the two lakes are hardly more than swamplands. Perhaps thousands of years ago the Okavango ran stronger.

Some authorities say that all of what is now Botswana might once have been covered by an enormous lake. One indication of this is seen in the Makarikari Salt Pans, a huge ancient lake bed about half as big

MAP KEY

Bobonong, D6
Botletle River, C3
Caprivi Strip, A2
Chobe Game Reserve, B4
Chobe River, A4
Debeeti, E5
Francistown, C5
Gaborone, E5
Ghanzi, D2
Hukuntsi, E2
Kalahari Desert, E2
Kalkfontein, D2

Kanye, F4
Kasane, A4
Khuis, G2
Kule, D1
Lake Ngami, C3
Lake Xau, C4
Lehututu, E2
Lephepe, E4
Limpopo River, D6
Lobatse, F4
Lokgwabe, E2
Mababe Depression, B4
Mafeking, F4

Mahalapye, E5
Makarikari (Salt Pans), C4
Marico River, E5
Maun, C3
Mochudi, E4
Mohembo, B2
Molepolole, E4
Molopo River, F3
Moshupa, E4
Nata, C5
Nata River, C5
Ngamiland, B2
Ngobe River, C3

Nossob River, F1
Notwani River, E4
Okavango River, A2
Okavango Swamps, B3
Old Tate, D6
Orapa, C4
Palapye, D5
Palla Road, E5
Pandamatenga, B4
Pickwe, D5
Rakoko, B3
Rakops, C4
Ramaquabane River, C6

Ramathlabama, F4
Ramoutsa, F4
Sepopa, B2
Serowe, D5
Seruli, D5
Shashi River, D6
Shushong, D5
Toteng, C3
Tsau, C2
Tshabong, F2
Tshane, E2
Tshwaane, D2
Zambezi River, A4

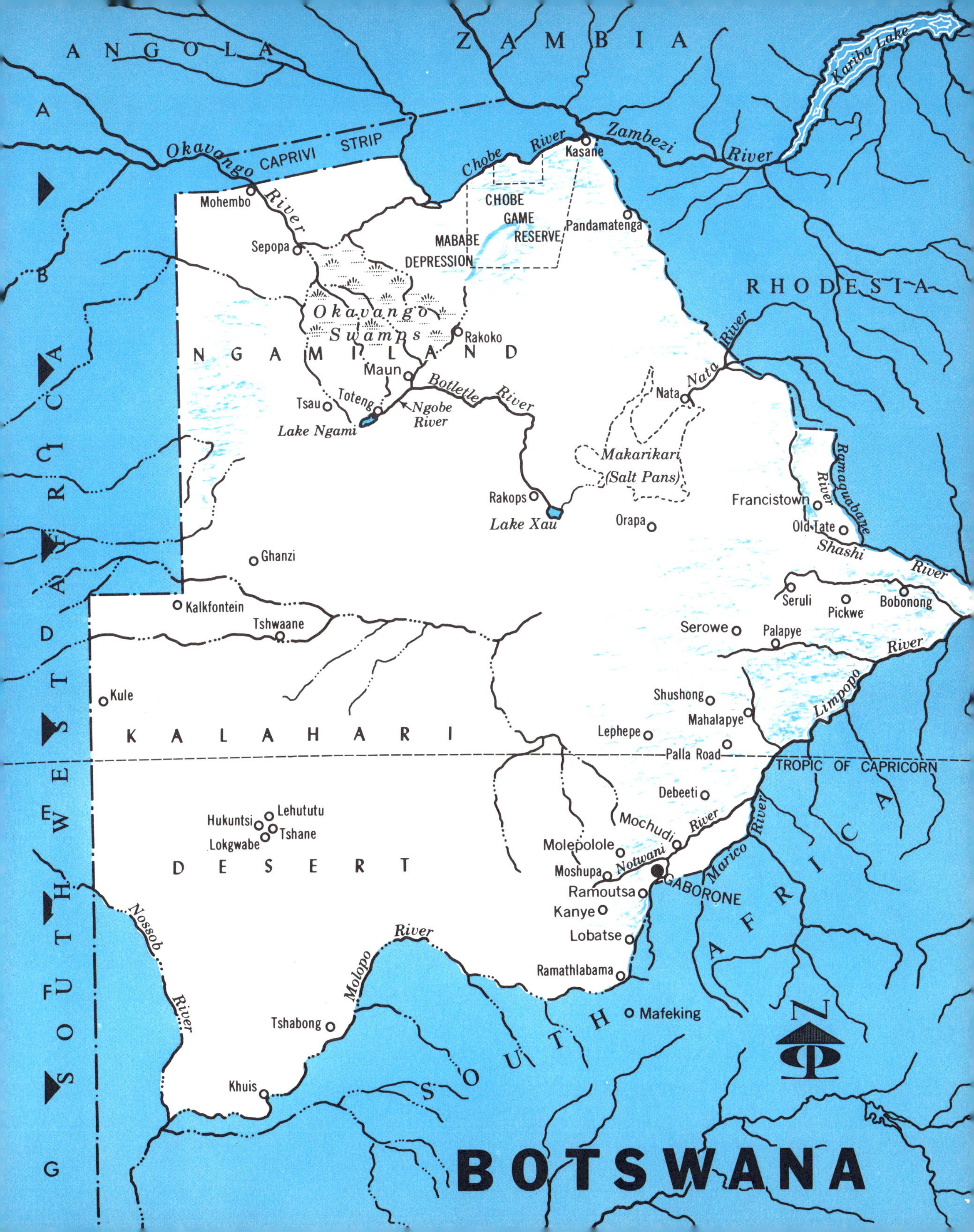
ANGOLA
ZAMBIA
Kariba Lake
Okavango
CAPRIVI STRIP
Chobe River
Kasane
Zambezi River
Mohembo
River
CHOBE GAME RESERVE
Pandamatenga
Sepopa
MABABE DEPRESSION
RHODESIA
Okavango Swamps
Rakoko
NGAMILAND
Maun
Nata River
Nata
Botlette River
Tsau
Toteng
Ngobe River
Lake Ngami
Makarikari (Salt Pans)
Ramaquabane River
Rakops
Lake Xau
Francistown
Orapa
Old Tate
Shashi River
Ghanzi
Kalkfontein
Seruli
Pickwe
Bobonong
Tshwaane
Serowe
Palapye
River
Kule
Shushong
Limpopo
Mahalapye
Lephepe
KALAHARI
Palla Road
TROPIC OF CAPRICORN
Debeeti
Lehututu
Hukuntsi
Tshane
Lokgwabe
Mochudi
River
Molepolole
Notwani
Marico River
DESERT
Moshupa
GABORONE
Ramoutsa
Kanye
Lobatse
Nossob River
Molopo River
Ramathlabama
Mafeking
Tshabong
Khuis
SOUTH AFRICA
SOUTH WEST AFRICA
BOTSWANA

as the Okavango Swamps. (The Makarikari is incorrectly marked on some maps as still being a lake.) Today the Makarikari is always dry, except for extremely rare times of flood when the Botletle River brings more water than Lake Xau can hold. Then the excess water runs off into the Salt Pans, but there is never enough to create more than small pools and puddles, which soon evaporate.

Lake Xau was first made known to outsiders by David Livingstone in 1851. He called it Lake Kumadow; *kuma* is a papyrus plant that clogged the lake then as it does even today, and *dow* (or *dau*) is a track, or path.

Lake Ngami is the only other natural lake in Botswana, and it is also a collector of draining swamp waters. Slightly smaller than Lake Xau, at floodtime it measures about five miles wide and twenty miles long.

A sign that northern Botswana once contained more water is the Mababe Depression, northeast of the Okavango Swamps. This shallow, thirty-mile-long hollow is completely dry. Once, like the Makarikari, it might have been a lake draining the swamps. When Livingstone explored more than a century ago, natives still lived near Mababe. Today, however, it is a dry and barren area vacated by man.

Botswana has many other rivers and streams, especially in the east where they flow into the Limpopo. Most of them are dry except in the rainy season or in flood

Except during floods, when the Okavango brings more water, Lake Ngami is mostly swamp.

Chobe River, one of the few rivers in Botswana that is always filled with water.

stage. It is not uncommon to see a borehole in the middle of a dry riverbed. Boreholes are dug throughout Botswana to provide drinking water. Some boreholes have pumps for raising the water. Unlike wells, which are permanent sources of water, boreholes often go dry.

The only rivers besides the Okavango that run year-round, even during droughts, are the Chobe (also called the Linyanti), the Limpopo (sometimes called the Crocodile), and the Marico.

Because Botswana is so arid, there are no forests. Much of the land is flat, part of the great plateau extending over much of south-central Africa. There are hills along the southeastern border and west and south of the Okavango Swamps. Although in places these hills reach as high as five thousand feet above sea level, they cannot accurately be called mountains since, for the most part, they are less than two thousand feet above ground level.

THE SANDS OF THE KALAHARI

Picture a desert with vast, empty wastes of sand, wind-arranged into gently curving dunes. Rain never falls; the sun beats down eternally; neither man nor animal nor plant can survive.

That is the picture of a true desert such as the Sahara in northern Africa, but it is not an accurate description of most of the Kalahari Desert. Only in extreme south-western Botswana does the Kalahari live up to the model of the Sahara, with dry, drifting dunes.

Most of the Kalahari—which means most of Botswana—is covered with clumps of grass that may grow as tall as a man, and with low, undersized scrub trees that seldom grow taller than twenty feet. This is the typical African bush country, well known throughout the world.

Vegetation grows on the Kalahari because, unlike most deserts, it does rain there, although seldom more than nine or ten inches a year. Rivers cross this desert, though they have no water except after a rain. Then for a few days—or perhaps even a few weeks—a trickle of water lies on the surface of the riverbeds and in a few scattered salt pans. Before long the water evaporates into the hot air or sinks into the sandy ground.

The occasional rain is enough to keep alive the many birds and animals that make their homes in the Kalahari. The native tribes of Botswana and most of the white settlers who arrived later have avoided this bleak area. Only the hardy Bushmen, the small, dark people who are taller than pygmies but shorter than most men, live there.

CLIMATE

Botswana lies below the equator, so it experiences winter when the Northern Hemisphere experiences summer. The Tropic of Capricorn passes through the

Only Bushmen live in the desert, carrying food and hunting equipment with them.

republic, giving it a subtropical climate.

In general, northern Botswana is warmer than southern Botswana. Temperatures above 100° F. are not uncommon in the north, where the mean maximum year-round temperature never drops below 75° F.

In winter the days are warm, but frosts are common in the north and may be severe in the southern desert. It has even been known to snow in the Kalahari, though the snow melts as it touches the ground.

Summer is the dry season; even in years without drought a rainfall between May and September is rare. Most of the rain falls between October and April; rainfall averages about twenty-five inches a year in the north and east, but no more than nine inches in the south.

Botswana is never harried by any of nature's severe tests such as earthquakes, volcanic eruptions, or tornadoes. The most violent storms to strike the country are the sporadic rainstorms during which rain falls so heavily for a short period that it washes away soil and plants and causes flash floods. Most precipitation comes in slow, steady rains quickly soaked up by the dry earth.

Nature's worst blows to Botswana are the periods when no rain falls at all. For years on end there may be drought, turning the land into a dustbowl. The latest drought, in the mid-1960s, lasted for five years. It killed one third of the cattle in Botswana. Various world relief organizations provided famine rations for the people and might very well have saved the entire population from certain death or from forced migration out of the area.

Children help themselves to food donated by world relief organizations during the long drought in the 1960s.

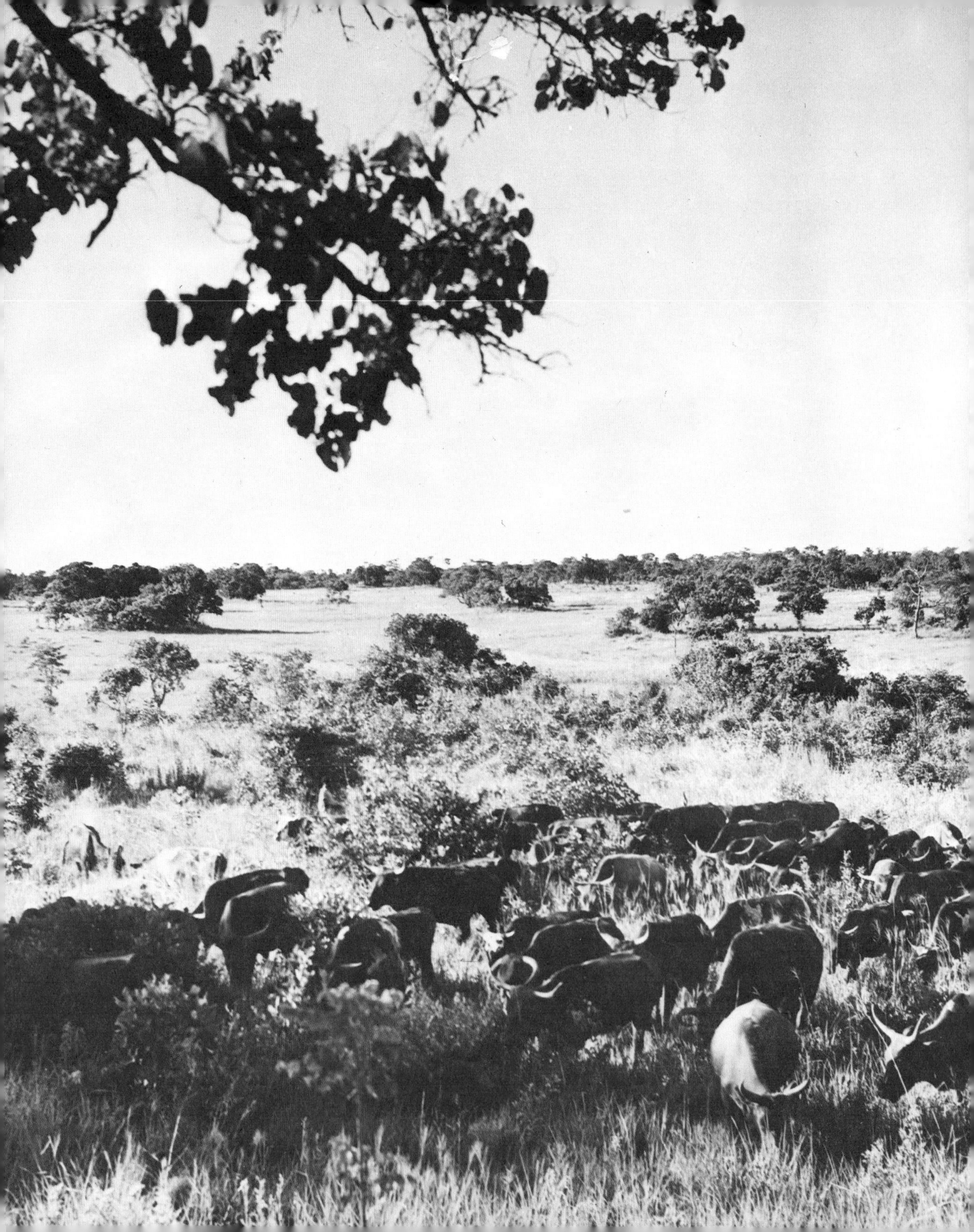

Three Children of Botswana

KENNETH OF SHUSHONG

Each of the several dozen cattle in the herd seems to be a different shade of brown. A few are light tan with a yellowish cast; some are so dark they seem to be purple. But most are in between—various shades of glossy hide ranging from a rich, russet brown to a dark, coppery hue.

The land on which the cattle graze has been used for no other purpose for generations. Several miles away, past a landscape of green, scrubby bushes and low, gnarled trees, is the village where the cattle are penned at night. Early each morning they are driven to the grazing spot by young boys of the village.

Each day Kenneth herds cattle to the grazing land several miles from his village.

BOTSWANA INFORMATION SERVICES

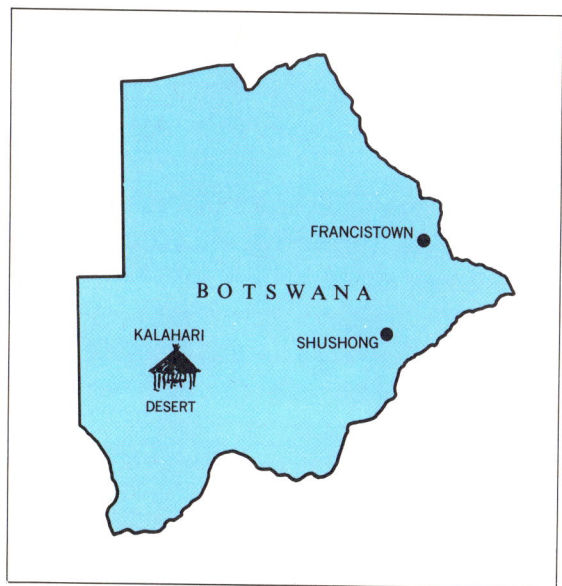

One of the boys, leaning against the bent trunk of a tree, is named Kenneth. He wears an old, tan shirt with the sleeves cut off just above the elbow and worn, tan shorts that come down to his knees. Kenneth notices that two of the cattle have wandered to the top of a small rise in the land several hundred yards away. With a shout, he runs to them and cuts them off. He uses a long, slender stick, flicking them on the sides and neck until they turn, moaning with protest, and slowly head back toward the rest of the herd.

The grazing land has no fences around it, because fences tend to indicate that individual people own the land, and this is banned by custom. Kenneth and the other boys spend each day as "living fences," watching the cattle feed and running to keep them together.

Unlike the grazing land, the cattle in the herd are owned by various individuals from the village. Kenneth knows which six belong to his father, but he also knows that the custom is for everyone to use the same grazing space, assigned by the chief of the tribe.

Several miles on the other side of the village is a small plot of land on which Kenneth's father raises crops for his family. His plot, too, has been assigned by the chief. When Kenneth's father dies, that same plot of farmland will most likely be passed down to Kenneth by the chief.

Little by little, the old tribal ways in Botswana are fading away. Fences are being erected and individual farmers are receiving leases or outright ownership to their own land. The modern ways that came to Botswana with independence in 1966 have yet to filter down to Kenneth's village.

New schools, too, are rising all over Botswana, but the nearest secondary school is more than fifty miles from Kenneth's village. The village does have a primary school, however, with about fifty students in the eight grades. Of the three teachers, only one has had any teacher's training. On days when the weather is fine, school meets outside, each class sitting on the ground under a different tree. Kenneth attended school for several years, until he started herding cattle for his father. Most of the children in Kenneth's village must start tending cattle and stop going to school before they finish eighth grade.

In a few years, when he is old enough to do a man's work, Kenneth wants to become a miner. As his father did, Kenneth will sign up to work in a diamond mine for a company in South Africa. His father has told him how the mine laborers travel to South Africa in a two-engine airplane. The plane trip will be the first time Kenneth has been more than ten or fifteen miles from his village.

Although he plans to work in the mines for just a few years, it is possible that Kenneth, like one of his uncles, might stay there for as long as twenty years. While he works, the mining company will put aside most of his wages and pay them to Kenneth after he returns home to Botswana.

Kenneth is fairly certain he will not decide to live in South Africa permanently. His father has described South Africa's *apartheid* (uh PAHR tayt) laws, which segregate the blacks from the whites. As a black mining worker, Kenneth's freedom would be restricted; he would not be able to go certain places or

Kenneth hopes that someday he will be able to visit Chobe Game Reserve.

do certain things. Even if he is unable to find a job when he returns to Botswana, at least he would be free to travel in his country as he pleases.

Someday Kenneth wants to visit the great game reserve in the north along the Chobe River. There is not much wild game left in the section of Botswana where Kenneth lives. He would like to sit on the banks of the river and watch the elephants and antelope and buffalo come and go, drinking from the river.

Eventually, Kenneth will probably become a farmer, as his father is. By the time he has a family, though, Kenneth hopes his own children will be able to attend both primary and secondary school. Perhaps they will be able to obtain good jobs in their own country.

KOPANO OF FRANCISTOWN

Kopano's dormitory room was built to hold ten boys, but twelve boys sleep in it. Early—very early—each morning the boys must make their beds and clean their room before a period of physical exercise outside. Breakfast is not served until after several classroom sessions have met. After breakfast are more classes, then a recess, followed by two more classes.

By this time the noon hour has passed, and the day has become too hot to sit inside. School is over for the day. After lunch, the rest of the afternoon is left for sports activities and meetings of school clubs such as the drama society, the singing choir, and the debate team. After supper, the students have time to study

Kopano's classes are often held outside.

and do homework inside in the school, which grows cooler as the sun goes down. Everyone must be in bed shortly after nine o'clock, when the lights go out for the day.

Kopano is in his first year of secondary school. He did not have to drop out of school early to become a cattle herder. His father is not a farmer, as are most of the men of Botswana, but is a medical technician. He travels with a team of other technicians and one doctor, treating people in outlying villages.

Kopano's school is in Francistown, one of the larger towns of eastern Botswana, about thirty miles from the village where he was born and grew up. It is a boarding school, which means Kopano and most of the other students live at the school during the week and travel home only on weekends and during vacations.

Kopano and his classmates dress like schoolchildren in any modern country in the world. The girls wear dresses or skirts and blouses, and the boys wear sport shirts and trousers. Their classrooms are large and airy, with blackboards, desks of wood and steel, and other up-to-date facilities.

The school was built less than five years ago, but already it is overcrowded. Although many children drop out of primary school, there are more children who want to attend secondary school than there are classrooms to hold them.

Kopano's studies include mathematics, history, English, veterinary science (girls take homemaking courses instead), and general science. He hopes someday to attend college. Though Botswana has no college or university of its own, it shares a joint university with two other small, former British protectorates, Lesotho and Swaziland. The university is located in Lesotho, a tiny republic surrounded by South Africa. With luck, and if he keeps his grades up, Kopano might be able to win a government scholarship to study there.

Kopano's father has traveled to many parts of Botswana through his work. He has discussed with Kopano some of the jobs that he could take after graduating from school if he is not able to attend college. He could work in the Civil Service in Gaborone, the capital city, or in some other large town. He could get a job as a veterinary inspector after further study at one of the government training schools or become a medical technician as his father is.

But Kopano enjoys the life at his school and wants to become a teacher. He would like to study at one of the governmental teacher-training centers. Few of the teachers in Botswana have college degrees, and many primary schoolteachers have very little training of any kind.

Kopano realizes that his young nation needs well-educated people to help it gain rank among the developing countries of Africa. As a teacher he would be doing much to assist his country toward that goal —and the work would be much more pleasant than laboring in an underground mine in some other country.

TIRA OF THE KALAHARI

Tira is nine years old and will surely marry within a year or two. Her husband will probably be almost twice her age, and he may be only the first of several husbands she will have. There will be no religious marriage ceremony. Her people believe in various kinds of spirits that live underground and in a good power in the sky that brings luck and good fortune to the tribe. When in her early teens, Tira will begin having children. She will probably have three or four in all, not counting the ones that die in infancy.

Tira is a girl of the Bushman tribes of the Kalahari Desert. Her language, Kloisan, has an unusual series of four or five different clicking sounds made with the tongue against the roof of the mouth. Using a few special symbols, Kloisan can be written in our alphabet, but it is difficult to do.

With the rest of the several dozen people of her small tribe, Tira wanders across the Kalahari looking for food and water. When her people settle in one spot for a while, they fashion "houses" from a few branches which lean together. This provides protection from the hot sun in the day and the cool winds at night. Since the desert often becomes very cold at night, the Bushmen cover themselves with animal skins and build fires for warmth. Each fire marks the area of an individual family. Some of the older people have scars on their bodies from having slept too close to the family fire.

At nine years, Tira is about three-and-one-half feet tall. As an adult, she may reach no more than an inch or two over four feet; the tallest member of her tribe measures only four feet, six inches. Like all other Bushmen, Tira has a split upper lip and a wide nose with little bridge.

With water so scarce on the desert, Tira is seldom able to wash or bathe. Under the hardened sand and clay, her skin has a yellowish tinge. When she was born, there was a dark spot at the bottom of her spine, but it is disappearing slowly as she grows older. No one has been able to explain the disappearing dark spot with which all Bushman children are born.

As do all of the people of her tribe, Tira wears nothing but a loincloth—a piece of animal skin hanging from a leather or woven cord around the waist—and sometimes another animal skin across her shoulders. In her tight, curly hair, she wears some beads made from the shells of bird eggs.

When Tira and her tribe have been without water for a long period of time, they move toward one of the boreholes that have been dug in the desert. Otherwise, about the only liquids drunk are those they find in wild plants and melons.

Bushmen are hunters and gatherers. Sixty to 70 percent of their food is wild berries, bird eggs, lizards, snakes, or insects—whatever the women can gather. Gathering activities take place almost every day. If anyone finds a large ostrich egg, the shell is saved. Water or other juices can be stored in it for drinking when needed.

Every day the men of Tira's tribe hunt with poisoned arrows.

BOTSWANA INFORMATION SERVICES

Tira and her friends often play ball in the sun.

If one of the men of the tribe is lucky enough to kill a wild antelope with a poisoned arrow, then the tribe can feast. Everyone, old and young, gets an equal share of the meat. It is heated in the coals of a fire started by one of the boys. He holds a dry stick steady on the ground with his feet. To it he touches the tip of an upright stick and twirls it fast between his palms. Soon a spark or two is struck and the fire is started.

Some of the people of Tira's tribe are able to find water under the desert sands. They dig a hole in the sand and poke the hollow stem of a plant into its damp bottom. They then suck up a muddy liquid through the stem. Spitting the liquid into their hand, they save it in the ostrich egg, where the sand sinks to the bottom.

When Tira and the other members of her tribe are happy, they hold dances. Only the men perform, doing complicated steps as they circle around a fire. The women and girls sing while seated, and their songs are as intricate and beautiful as the dance steps the men do.

It is not likely that Tira will ever see a town or attend a school or know what it is to have fresh drinking water every day. Some of the Bushmen of the Kalahari Desert in Botswana have moved to the edge of society. They wear clothing, live in one place all the time, and sometimes even work for people who own cattle ranches.

Before the twentieth century is over, the Bushmen will probably have been integrated into the rest of the life of Botswana.

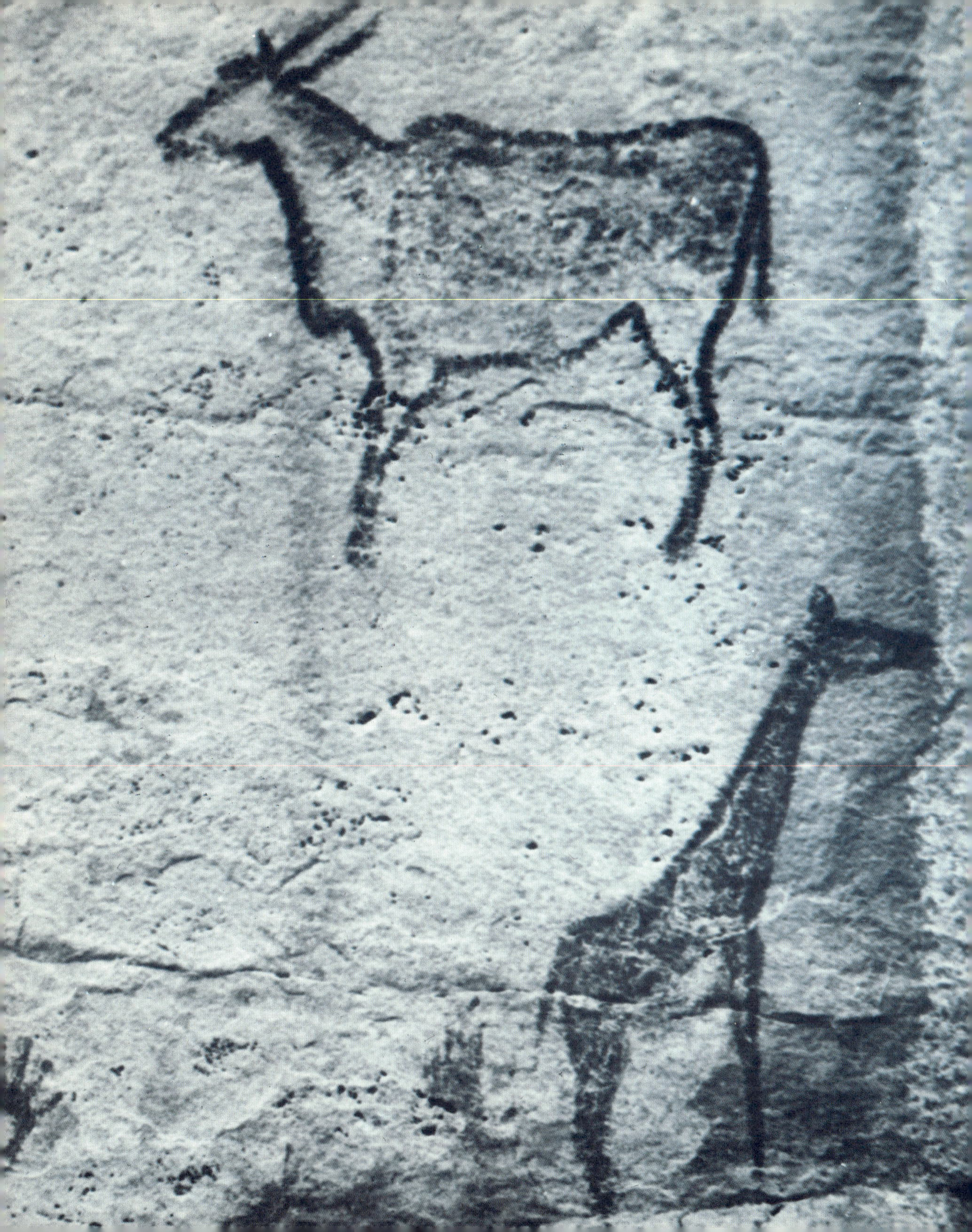

Botswana Yesterday

MEN OF TSWANA

Prehistoric times are those years before history was written down, before it was saved for future generations to read and learn about. African history, which dates back to prehistoric times, has been passed by word-of-mouth from parent to child through many generations.

Botswana's modern historic times began when Europeans first explored and settled there, at the start of the nineteenth century. This was several decades after the United States of America had declared its independence from Great Britain.

The native tribes found by the first Europeans in what is now Botswana were called the Batswana. They are said to have migrated southward from near the equator several centuries before—no one knows exactly when, but 1600 is usually the latest date given. It is thought that the tribes pushed the smaller Bushmen people ahead of them in their slow progress south. Eventually the Bushmen took refuge in the Kalahari Desert, where they remain today. The Batswana did not want to enter such a desolate area. Some anthropologists think the Kalahari Bushmen might be the only remaining members of a once large population.

According to Batswana legend, the gods who created the world came out of the earth. In eastern Botswana are footprints

Bushman paintings such as these found in northwestern Botswana show that Bushmen once lived in that area.

BOTSWANA INFORMATION SERVICES

of men and animals in a rock hardened thousands of years ago from the molten lava of some unknown volcanic catastrophe. The Batswana believed those prints were made by the first creatures on earth.

By 1800 there were eight main tribes of the native group called Batswana, plus several smaller tribes that at some time or another had broken away and set up councils of their own. Legend states that the first Batswana tribe was founded by a man named Masilo. His three sons, Kwena, Ngwato, and Ngwaketse, are said to have headed the three tribes called Bakwena, Bamangwato (sometimes called Bangwato), and Bangwaketse.

Most Batswana tribes were named after chiefs, as were the three mentioned above. "Ba" means "men of"; thus, "Batswana" means "men of the Tswana." The other five main Tswana tribes are the Batawana, Bakgatla, Batlokwa, Barolong (sometimes called Barolonga), and Bamalete.

The Batswana originally settled farther south than what is today the southern border of Botswana. In the early 1800s they were driven back by fierce warriors of the Zulu tribes, who then controlled much of the territory below the Limpopo and Molopo rivers.

The Dutch were the first white men to settle in the land below those rivers, today the Republic of South Africa. Though the Dutch, and later the British, searched for diamonds, gold, and other treasures in southern Africa, they did not penetrate far enough into Africa to reach what is now Botswana.

DR. LIVINGSTONE

The first European to enter the land of the Zulu-Batswana wars was Robert Moffat, a representative of the London Missionary Society. In 1820 he founded a village at the present-day town of Kuruman, among Batswana natives who had remained south of the Molopo. (Today Kuruman is in South Africa.) For some unknown reason, Moffat's mission was not raided by the rampaging Matabele, a tribe of Zulus fighting the Batswana in that area.

By 1840 the British controlled most of the southern tip of Africa, while the Dutch had moved northward to the Transvaal, the territory south of the Limpopo River. The Dutch, called Boers (a Dutch word meaning "farmers"), wanted the rich mineral and diamond mines of the Transvaal for themselves. They tried to prevent the British from moving northward, and continually made raids on a "missionary" road the British had built from the Cape of Good Hope, at the southern tip of Africa, to the land of the Batswana.

In 1841 in the midst of the endless disagreements, raids, and battles between the Matabele and Batswana tribes and between the Boers and British, another white man arrived. This man also came as a representative of the London Missionary Society; in fact, he had married Robert Moffat's daughter. A Scotsman who eventually became more famous as an explorer than as a missionary, David Livingstone stayed in Bechuanaland for a dozen years.

Top: Livingstone visits the dying Sebituane, chief of one of the Batswana tribes. Bottom: After founding a village at what is now Kuruman, Moffat crossed the Zambezi River in a ferry.

President Seretse Khama (third from left) and Lady Khama (second from left) visit the ruins of the old London Missionary Society Church at Palapye in 1970.

BOTSWANA INFORMATION SERVICES

In the 1840s Livingstone settled with the Bakwena tribe and eventually converted their chief, Sechele, to Christianity. Livingstone's home was in a town near present-day Gaborone. Today, more than 130 years later, the London Missionary Society still has missionaries living and preaching in this region. Livingstone is still remembered as a good man who did much to help the Bakwena.

Livingstone took the side of the Bakwena against the Transvaal Boers, who had been raiding the natives and the British missionary road from the Cape. By this time the Transvaal and the territory known as the Orange Free State were no longer influenced by the British Cape Colony at the southern tip of Africa. Livingstone asked the British colonial authorities back home for help in his work, but the official policy at that time was not to expand or obtain new colonies.

Livingstone was typical of the hardy European missionaries of the last half of the nineteenth century who devoted their lives to taking Christianity to the natives of Africa. Many years later, after his stay in Bechuanaland and after given up for dead, Livingstone was found in what is now Tanzania by Henry M. Stanley, a British explorer sent by a newspaper from New York City to find what had become of the courageous Scottish missionary.

In 1866, after Livingstone had moved northward, gold was discovered in the Tati region of Bechuanaland, named after the

Tati River. The Boers immediately pushed over from the Transvaal, claimed the Tati region, and forced out the Bamangwato tribe living there. Though the Boers had the Tati gold mines and had cut the northern road (which by then extended into present-day Rhodesia), the British still refused to listen to the pleas of missionaries to annex Bechuanaland.

KHAMA THE GREAT

The natives of Bechuanaland needed a strong, powerful person to lead their resistance to the encroaching Boers. As so often happens in history, the right man appeared in the right place at the right time.

His name was Khama III, but he also became known as Khama the Great. He inherited the chieftainship of the Bamangwato tribe from his father in the mid-1870s. As a boy, Khama was converted to Christianity by the missionaries. As a chief, he followed their advice and prohibited alcoholic drinks, built schools, and caused his people to drop some of their traditional customs.

Though the eight tribes of the Batswana had often fought among themselves, it was not long before Khama organized them into one powerful force. Not only did he finally put an end to the warfare with the Matabele, but he also did much to unify the natives of Bechuanaland so they would not allow Europeans to take over their country, as had happened in many other parts of Africa.

THREE GREAT AFRICAN CHIEFS

Chief of the Bamangwato, Khama the Great was one of the three most powerful chiefs in the history of Bechuanaland. He united the native tribes and ended the fighting with the Matabele.

Khama needed help in fighting the Boers, some of whom were starting to cross Bechuanaland to settle in South West Africa, west of Bechuanaland. He appealed to Britain for aid in holding off the Boers, with the unwritten understanding that he and the other chiefs would continue to rule Bechuanaland.

In response to this appeal, the British met in 1881 with the Boers at the city of Pretoria in the Transvaal. They set the Limpopo River as a border across which the Boers were not to settle. Because no attempt was made to enforce this so-called Pretoria Convention, the Boer raids continued.

A UNIQUE COLONY

In the next few years, many Germans settled in what is now South West Africa. With the Germans to the west and Dutch Boers to the east, Britain was afraid it would be squeezed out and would no longer have a road north through Bechuanaland to central Africa.

Another meeting was held in an effort to solve the problem. The London Convention of 1884 again set up a border between the Transvaal and Bechuanaland, almost exactly the same one agreed on in 1881. When Boers raided the town of Mafeking, just below the Molopo River in Bechuanaland, the British sent a force headed by General Charles Warren to push them out. Khama and the other Batswana chiefs welcomed Warren, feeling that British aid was better than German or Dutch domination.

In 1885 the land below present-day Botswana became part of the Cape Colony and was known as British Bechuanaland. Today this land is part of South Africa. The territory north of the Molopo to 22° south latitude became the Bechuanaland Protectorate. (In 1892 it was enlarged to the northern boundaries of present-day Botswana.)

Aside from keeping the Germans and the Dutch out of the protectorate and keeping the road north to Rhodesia open, the British were not interested in this region. They relied on the Batswana chiefs to control the protectorate.

This made a unique situation in the land of the Batswana. White men controlled, or "protected," the protectorate, but they generally let the natives alone. The tribal chiefs continued to enforce the traditional laws and customs of the people. In contrast, the natives of other southern Africa colonies were completely dominated by white settlers; as in many places today, small white minorities ruled the huge black majorities.

CECIL RHODES

In 1889 a business firm called the British South Africa Company was granted a charter to all mining rights in the Cape Colony, in land north of the Transvaal, and in what is now Botswana. The company was headed by Cecil Rhodes. Rhodes wanted to push the Boers from the rich mining lands of the Transvaal, to keep them from entering present-day Rhodesia, and to control the Bechuanaland Protectorate.

Khama III and the other native chiefs were horrified. Their British "protectors" were about to hand over their land to a company that would be certain to exploit them and take away their power. Khama especially feared the possibility that the company would introduce alcoholic drinks to his tribal area. With two other chiefs,

Head of the British South Africa Company was Cecil Rhodes. Rhodes often said that he preferred the bushland of southern Africa to banquets in London.
Above: Rhodes (left) with his secretary and his valet.
Left: One of the last photographs taken of Rhodes.

Khama traveled to London in 1895 to plead the case before the British government. They were received by Queen Victoria with dignity and pomp, but their pleas against the company charter were ignored.

Rhodes never succeeded in taking over the Bechuanaland Protectorate. His mighty thirst for power caused his company to lose its rights in that area. In December, 1895, with Rhodes's approval but without the approval of the British government, a group of British settlers in the protectorate raided the Boer town of Johannesburg in the Transvaal. The British government realized that it would have to keep control of the protectorate to prevent such dangerous actions. Above all, it wanted to avoid a war with the Dutch.

While Rhodes was in charge, however, the three most powerful chiefs of Bechuanaland had each been forced to cede a block of land along the eastern border of the protectorate, where Rhodes wanted to build a railroad north to Rhodesia. When his company lost its rights in the protectorate, these blocks were not returned to the chiefs but were administered by the British instead. Later they were given back to the British South Africa Company for settlement by Europeans and for building the railroad. They are known as the Lobatse, Gaborone, and Tuli blocks and remain the three major centers of white population in Botswana today.

Many white people also still live in the Tati Concession farther north, where they had originally been attracted to gold mines that soon ran out, and in the Ghanzi District near the border with South West Africa, originally settled by Boers from Transvaal with Rhodes's approval.

By the turn of the century the Bechuanaland Protectorate was divided much as it remained until independence. In the five centers of white settlement—the three blocks, the Tati Concession, and the Ghanzi district—British commissioners held rule. There were various native tribal areas where the chiefs and native courts were in charge, and there were the so-called Crown Lands, mostly unpopulated regions of the extreme northwest and the Kalahari Desert.

Until independence, the entire Bechuanaland Protectorate was administered by a British commissioner in the town of Mafeking, south of the Molopo River. This is one of the few examples in world history of a capital city being situated outside the boundaries of its territory.

TWO WARS

War finally broke out between the British and the Dutch. From 1899 to 1902, the British fought the Dutch of the Transvaal and Orange Free State colonies in what is known as the Boer, or South African, War. When the Boers finally lost, the British decided to unite all of their possessions in southern Africa into one giant colony—to be called the Union of South Africa. The chiefs of Bechuanaland and two other British protectorates, Swaziland

and Basutoland (Lesotho today), did not want to become part of this Union. They feared that their tribes, like other tribes in British and Dutch colonies, would lose all of their land and rights.

Britain agreed to let the three protectorates remain as they were, but insisted that someday the three would have to join the Union of South Africa.

After the defeat of the Germans in World War I, the Union of South Africa received a mandate from the newly-formed League of Nations to administer South West Africa, formerly a German colony. Some Botswana natives had worked with the South African Army in World War I. By this time Southern Rhodesia (Rhodesia today) and Northern Rhodesia (Zambia today) were also controlled by the British. Bechuanaland was surrounded by British colonies.

The British still were not much interested in the little protectorate, since no rich mineral deposits had been discovered there. Mainly they kept charge to keep other nations out and to keep control of the completed railroad that passed through the eastern edge of Bechuanaland.

THE POWER OF THE CHIEFS

From time to time the British intervened in various aspects of the natives' self-rule. Certain disagreements between tribes and quarrels about borders made it seem necessary for them to step in and calm down matters. As much as they wanted to leave Bechuanaland alone, the British at times found it necessary to act in order to protect the rights of certain people or tribes in the protectorate, or merely to keep peace.

In doing so, the British discovered that the Batswana actually had little say in their tribal governments. Their chiefs ruled over them as autocratic kings whose word was law. The councils, or *kgotlas,* of the tribes actually had very little power. Tribal members were permitted to farm plots of land, but they could not own the land.

In 1920 the British set up a Native Advisory Council, later called the African Council, made up of representatives of the kgetlas. Although the British Resident Commissioner had the final say in council decisions, at least members of the tribes now had a chance to voice their opinions about matters dealing with their interests.

At the same time, a European Advisory Council was organized; it represented the white residents and farmers of Bechuanaland. Like the Native Council, the European Advisory Council could only advise the commissioner—in this case, regarding laws and regulations concerning whites in the protectorate. Many whites wanted to join the Union of South Africa, which would mean an end to the native self-rule; thus, the British government undertook a study of Bechuanaland to determine what changes needed to be made.

In 1933 the Pim Report on the government of Bechuanaland recommended that the power of the chiefs be defined more clearly, and, in fact, be reduced—especially concerning the role of the chiefs as heads of native courts. The report also indicated that the white administration of the protectorate might be more effective if it were allied with the Union of South Africa.

The chiefs opposed both reform proposals. The most powerful chief at the time was another head of the Bamangwato. After his death in 1923, Khama III had been succeeded by his son, Sekgoma. When Sekgoma died only two years later, the chieftainship fell to his son, Seretse, who was only four years old. Until Seretse came of age, the Bamangwato were led by the chief's uncle, Khama III's youngest son, Tshekedi Khama.

As *regent* (a person who rules until the real ruler comes of age), Tshekedi, like his father, ruled with strict benevolence. At one time he shocked the British of southern Africa by trying a white man on a morals charge, finding him guilty, and ordering him to be flogged. This unheard-of punishment of a white man by a black man caused an uproar. A detachment of the British Royal Navy was ordered into Bamangwato tribal land. Though Tshekedi was deposed by the British, he returned to power as soon as the navy left.

Despite the protests of Tshekedi and other chiefs, the Native Administration and Native Tribunal Proclamations of 1934 severely regulated their power. For the first time they were ordered to obey the directions of the British commissioner. No longer did the kgotlas, which followed the chiefs' advice, have judicial power over the natives. Instead, native laws were to be judged by separate native courts with definite powers.

Tshekedi sued the commissioner for this infringement of the chiefs' hereditary powers, but lost the case in a special British court ruling. The chiefs, however, did win one of their battles against proposals of the Pim Report.

The British government declared that Bechuanaland would not become part of the Union of South Africa unless the natives of the protectorate approved. Considering the plight of blacks in colonies surrounding Bechuanaland where blacks were kept in virtual slavery by the white minorities, such approval would hardly be forthcoming.

A NEW LOOK

A new British commissioner was sent to the capital at Mafeking in 1936. Unlike earlier administrators, Charles Arden-Clarke was sympathetic to the needs and the rights of the natives. Realizing Arden-Clarke could help them, Tshekedi and other chiefs cooperated fully with him.

Despite protests from the whites of South Africa, Arden-Clarke in 1938 set up tribal treasuries to collect taxes from members of the tribes. The tax treasuries, supervised by native committees, were used to improve the education and farming methods of each tribe. Tshekedi used the treasury of the Bamangwato to build the first secondary school for blacks in Bechuanaland—Moeng College.

The chiefs were able to reassert their own power and that of their kgotlas in 1943 when new proclamations replaced those of 1934. The result was to make cooperation between the British and the natives in Bechuanaland better than in any other protectorate or colony.

The whites of southern Africa were horrified at the British government's concessions to the Batswana people. They realized that education, improved farming, and judicial power might someday give the blacks of Bechuanaland the desire to run their own country independently. Such a precedent could ruin the white control of southern Africa.

During World War II, about ten thousand members of the Batswana tribes served with the British African Pioneer Corps in Italy, northern Africa, and the Middle East. They were recruited by traditional tribal calls to war, with the chiefs "requesting" that their men take arms against the enemies of the British. As in World War I, Batswanans worked mainly as laborers, since British army units were not racially integrated at the time.

The chieftainship of a Batswana tribe had always been a powerful position; chiefs were even considered supreme by their tribes. In the pichos, *public meetings, chiefs would speak to their tribe about how its government was being run. The power of the chiefs was greatly reduced, however, through various British moves beginning in 1920. It was not until 1943 that proclamations were announced, enabling the chiefs to reassert their power.*

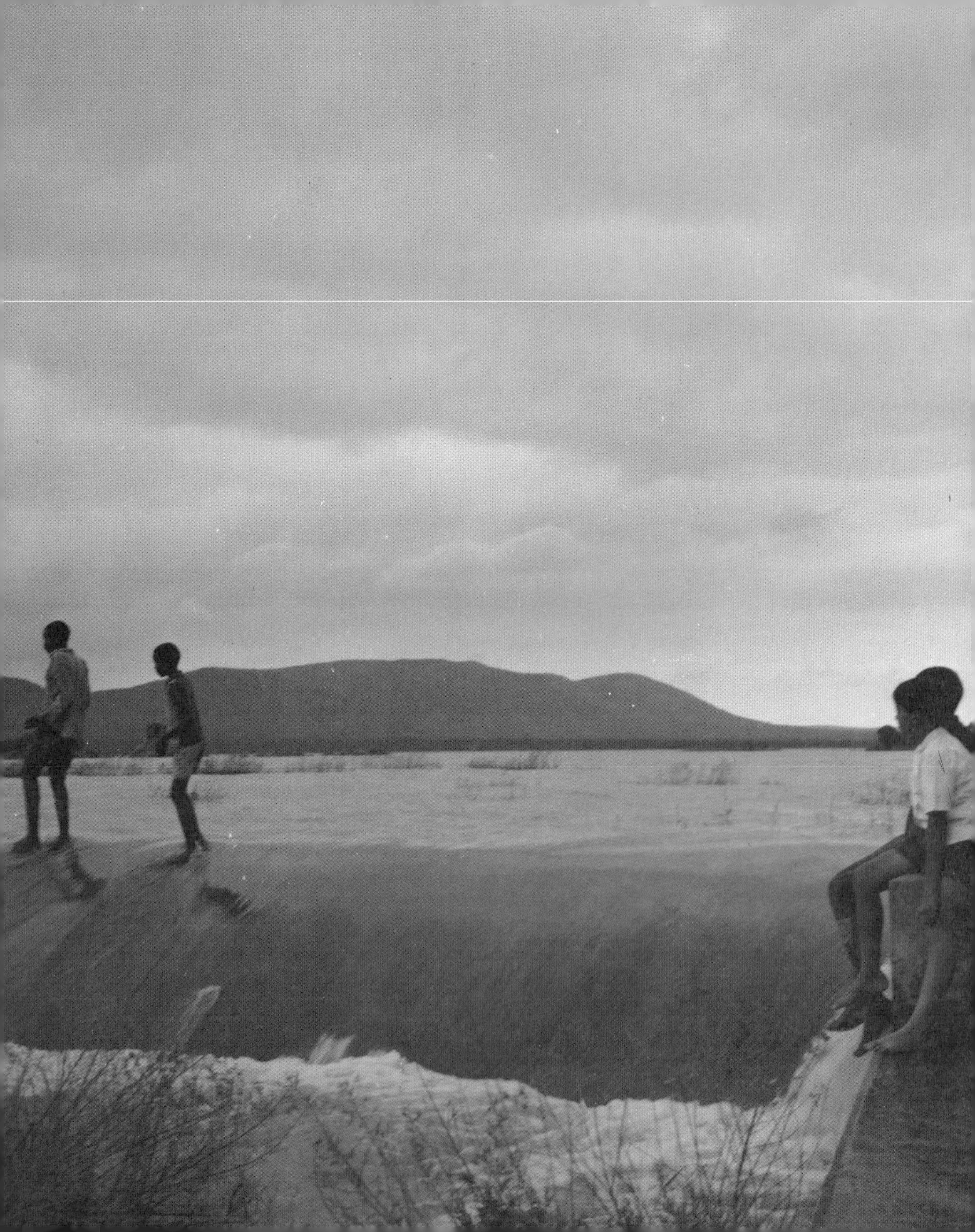

Botswana Today

LOVE AND MARRIAGE

In the immediate post-World War II period, Tshekedi again enraged the Union of South Africa by complaining publicly that it was about to swallow up South West Africa. Britain prevented Tshekedi from traveling to the United Nations to present his appeal, and that international body did nothing to prevent the South African takeover.

South Africa's racial policy in South West Africa was the same one it practiced at home. Called *apartheid,* this policy enforces separation between the minority ruling whites and the great masses of blacks. The latter have no voting rights, have few job or educational opportunities, and are forced to live in certain sections of cities and, in some cases, only in certain portions of the nation.

Soon after the war, Seretse Khama, the young chief of the Bamangwato, became old enough to rule the tribe officially, replacing his regent-uncle, Tshekedi, Seretse, however, asked that his installation as chief be postponed until he could obtain a law degree from Oxford University in England. While at Oxford, Seretse fell in love with a white woman named Ruth Williams; they were married in 1948.

Often families of all races can be seen enjoying themselves at Gaborone Dam. Though Botswana is bordered by nations that practice apartheid, discrimination is a minor and less disruptive force in Botswana. The ideal that the Batswana have for their country is a state in which all races can live and work in harmony.

MICHAEL ROBERTS

39

The marriage caused international attention. In Southern Africa, whites feared it might set an example for future interracial marriages in that part of the world. Though some of the Bamangwato remained loyal to their hereditary chief, Tshekedi and many other Bamangwato believed Seretse should not be allowed to assume the throne. They had three reasons: Seretse had not asked for permission to marry, as tribal custom dictated; future chiefs of the tribe (Seretse's heirs) would not be full-blooded Bamangwato; and later, when Seretse and his wife had twins, they argued that twins had long been considered an unlucky sign in the tribe.

The Bamangwato kgotla, headed by Tshekedi, could not agree on whether to allow Seretse to assume the chieftainship. It first voted against him, then reversed itself and took his side. Finally the British government, pressured by South Africa, stepped in. Seretse was exiled to London and Tshekedi was forced to leave the Bamangwato lands. An acting chief was named by the kgetla to head the embattled tribe; he was later replaced by a ruling committee.

EXILE AND RETURN

In exile with the Bakwena tribe, Tshekedi continued his campaign to bring progress to all of the people of Bechuanaland. In 1951 the British combined their two advisory councils into a Joint Advisory Council representing both blacks and whites. Tshekedi was named to

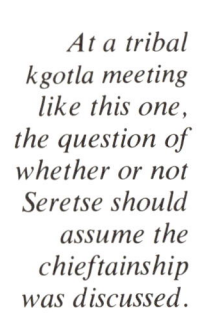

At a tribal kgotla meeting like this one, the question of whether or not Seretse should assume the chieftainship was discussed.

the new council by the chief of the Bakwena. Even in exile, he was an important leader.

In 1954 South Africa again tried to take control of the three protectorates, Bechuanaland, Swaziland, and Basutoland. The British government, headed by Sir Winston Churchill, again insisted this could not be done unless the people of those territories agreed to annexation. Tshekedi argued that without a voice in legislative matters, his people could never let the British know how they felt on any subject. He wanted a native legislative council with power to pass laws to replace the Joint Advisory Council.

In order to placate the Bamangwato, Tshekedi's exile was revoked by the British in 1952. He was allowed to return to Bamangwato land as a private citizen.

Four years later Tshekedi went to London and was reunited with his nephew. He convinced Seretse to renounce his claim and the claims of his heirs to the chieftainship of the Bamangwato. When Seretse did this, the British revoked Seretse's exile. Uncle and nephew returned to Bamangwato land, where both lived quietly as common members of the tribe—one a former regent-chief, the other a former chief only in name.

In June of 1959 Tshekedi died. He was mourned throughout Bechuanaland as a man who had devoted his entire life to his people. Khama the Great and Tshekedi Khama are still remembered as the two greatest chiefs who ever led a Batswana tribe.

When he died, Tshekedi believed that his nephew, the rightful chief of the Bamangwato, would never serve in that position, having renounced his claim. What he could not know was that in a few years Seretse would hold a position more powerful than any Batswana chief could imagine.

NEW PARTIES

Had Tshekedi lived a short while longer, he would have seen his dream of a legislative council come true. On December 6, 1960, the British announced the formation of legislative and executive councils, to include both elected and appointed members of both black and white races. The first legislative council met on June 21, 1961, in Lobatse and began to plan the protectorate's first constitution.

This was the first truly British step toward giving Bechuanaland a government of its own. At the same time, the Union of South Africa had resigned from the British Commonwealth. Calling itself the Republic of South Africa, the new nation enforced even harsher restrictions against blacks. Many blacks sought refuge across the border in Bechuanaland. Their presence there reinforced the protectorate's fear of South Africa and its racial policy.

The year 1960 saw more than a dozen African nations north of Bechuanaland declaring or receiving their independence. Across the continent swept a surge toward freedom that could not be stopped by the

European countries that had colonized Africa. Only in several Portuguese colonies and in southern Africa were the white minorities to remain in power for long.

In Bechuanaland the first whispers of a desire for independence from the British began to circulate. With Tshekedi gone, there were no strong tribal or political leaders to guide the protectorate. Before 1960, there were not even any political parties.

The first political front, organized in December, 1960, was the Bechuanaland People's Party. It was founded by Kgeleman T. Motsete, a Bamangwato educated in England and prominent in promoting education in Bechuanaland. Motsete's party called for independence, for black control of the protectorate, and for the end of any white representation in government.

Before long, various factions split the People's Party. In 1964 Motsete was replaced as leader by P. Matante, who was even more radical in calling for immediate black power and the ousting of the whites. A small group of party members, headed by Motsamai Mpho, broke off and formed the Independence Party.

CALL FOR INDEPENDENCE

After his uncle's death, Seretse Khama began to take an active part in his country's politics. He was backed by members of the Bamangwato tribe, many of whom still considered him their uncrowned chief, and by other natives in the protectorate. Seretse was elected to the Legislative Council and later to the Executive Council.

As were his grandfather and uncle, Seretse was a peaceful man who felt that his people would not be able to obtain their rights through violent or radical means. Opposed to the nationalistic program of the People's Party, in 1962 he formed the Bechuanaland Democratic Party. The party immediately had a large following, since Seretse was supported by the largest tribe in Bechuanaland, the Bamangwato.

Though the Democratic Party also called for independence, it did not have an antiwhite platform as did the People's Party. Seretse insisted that all white residents in Bechuanaland should be able to vote and have a voice in the government. He realized, of course, that since blacks outnumbered whites, under ordinary circumstances, an equal vote would not give the whites great political power.

Meanwhile, Matante had been appearing before the United Nations, protesting the British colonial treatment of the protectorate. Addressing a crowd of his People's Party followers late in 1962 in Francistown, Matante helped to cause a disturbance that had to be subdued with tear gas.

The British government was amazed by this sudden outbreak in a colony where only two years before no one had spoken of independence. The British commissioner and other white leaders believed

Left: Though exiled by the British government, Seretse Khama was still considered the uncrowned chief of the Bamangwato tribe by many of its members. Below: Seretse speaks to five thousand people at a tribal meeting in Ngamiland.

that although Bechuanaland was not yet prepared for freedom, there was little they could do to slow its coming. They announced that in 1963 the constitution would be reviewed "with a view to further political advance."

A NEW CONSTITUTION

A conference on the new constitution began at Lobatse in July, 1963. Those present included the commissioner (representing the British government), representatives from the tribes, the political parties, and the white European community. In November the commissioner announced plans for internal self-rule.

Elections were to be held in 1965 for a new Legislative Assembly, representing both whites and blacks on a one-man, one-vote basis. The Assembly would elect a prime minister and cabinet as leaders of the protectorate; they would hold the majority of political power, with only a few powers reserved for the commissioner. The Assembly would refer all matters regarding tribal authority to a new House of Chiefs.

The British government also proclaimed a five-year plan designed to put Bechuanaland on a self-supporting economic basis so it would not have to depend so much on Britain for aid. Though grants were approved to help farmers and traders, new schools were planned, and

Until shortly before independence, Gaborone was only a sleepy village. Today it is a major rail center and the major town in Botswana.

MICHAEL ROBERTS

loans were floated to build roads and improve communications, five years seemed a very short time in which to change a quiet, landlocked protectorate into a thriving, independent republic, economically able to stand on its own feet.

Perhaps most important of all—at least symbolically—a new capital city was planned. If the protectorate were to become an independent republic, it could hardly continue to have its capital city outside its boundaries at Mafeking. It was decided to locate the capital at the little town of Gaborone, on the railroad that cut through the protectorate. The change was made officially in February, 1965.

WHITE RESENTMENT

Most of the whites of Bechuanaland were farmers, cattle ranchers, and businessmen. They were British, South African, or Dutch, whose ancestors had come from the Transvaal. Almost all of them opposed independence, fearing the integration and loss of white power that would result from it.

After a group of Dutch farmers in the Tati Concession tried unsuccessfully to secede from Bechuanaland, they sought help elsewhere, first from the white governments of South Africa and Southern Rhodesia, then from the United Nations. The radical Independence Party reacted to this by insisting that whites should not be allowed to own any land in the future independent republic.

In the Ghanzi district, white farmers withdrew their children from schools in 1964 when desegregation in classrooms was banned by the government. Some of the white protest was stilled late in 1964 when two bills were passed banning any sort of racial discrimination.

PLANNING THE ELECTION

As the elections of 1965 neared, plans were hurriedly put into effect. Before election districts could be laid out, each with an approximately equal number of voters, a national census was held. Everyone was counted, except for some of the wandering Bushmen of the Kalahari.

To the surprise of all, the final count showed many more people in Bechuanaland than had been suspected. Early in the 1960s, estimates of the total population were near the figure of 330,000. The 1964 census showed the population to be 543,105.

Voter registration began in September, 1964. Voters had to be twenty-one years old, British subjects or British "protected persons" (the natives), and either native-born or residents for at least one year. Those whites of Dutch ancestry who had not become British citizens were not allowed to vote, which led them to protest.

More than two hundred registration points were set up around the country. Since many of the prospective voters could not read, each political party was given a color and a symbol, which would be reproduced on the ballots. The symbol for Seretse's Democratic Party was an automobile jack. The Boer word for jack is *domkraag,* which is as close as many natives could come to pronouncing the word "democratic."

VICTORY FOR SERETSE

About 75 percent of the registered voters went to the polls on March 1, 1965. The day had the appearance of a national holiday, since the people were, in fact, celebrating their first opportunity to cast ballots.

Seretse's Democratic Party won a remarkable victory at the polls, receiving more than 123,000 votes, or more than six times as many votes as the runner-up People's Party. Part of the success was a personal triumph for Seretse, whose moderate manner and quiet bearing appealed to a majority of the people. Just as important was the fact that the voters had rejected the harsh antiwhite tactics of Seretse's political rivals and had chosen instead the nonradical, nondiscriminatory, nonviolent path toward independence.

The Democratic Party won twenty-eight seats in the new Legislative Assembly, leaving only three seats to the People's Party. As leader of the winning party, Seretse was asked by the British commissioner to become prime minister of the protectorate. The new prime minister announced that full independence for his country would arrive in only eighteen months, and that after independence it would remain a part of the British Commonwealth.

Seretse also announced that Bechuanaland would be known as the Botswana Protectorate until independence and that after complete withdrawal of the British government, it would become the Republic of Botswana.

Seretse took immediate steps to enter into friendly relations with the Republic of Zambia, the only neighboring country governed by blacks. This nation, formerly Northern Rhodesia, had gained its independence in 1964. Seretse remained cool toward South Africa and Rhodesia. Late in 1965 the latter suddenly declared its independence from Britain and became a white-controlled republic much like South Africa. Surprisingly, the government of South Africa had neither denounced Seretse nor the new government of Botswana, despite their differences of racial policy.

THE EIGHTEEN MONTHS

On March 23, 1965, three weeks after the election, Botswana's first Legislative Assembly met. Since the governmental buildings at the new capital, Gaborone, had not been completed, the Assembly was opened at Lobatse in the home of the British High Court.

With much to do in the eighteen months before complete independence, Seretse and his government were faced with two major problems. The first concerned the periodic droughts that strike the country. Because the drought of the 1960s lasted for five years, it ruined the chances for success of the five-year plan designed to bring about Botswana's economic independence. Almost one third of the 1.3 million head of cattle in the protectorate died from the drought or were slaughtered because they could not be fed and watered. This was practically a death blow to Botswana's only industry, the sale of cattle and meat.

Food crops would not grow in the dried soil, and a great number of people were threatened by famine. It is estimated that more than 60 percent of the people would have perished had it not been for food shipments sent by the United Nations and British relief organizations. South Africa was not asked for, and did not offer, any assistance.

At the same time, Prime Minister Seretse faced a surge of old and new political rivals determined to grasp power before Botswana reached independence. A new political party, the Botswana National Front, was organized by Kenneth Koma, who had been ejected from South Africa as a communist. Educated in Britain and Russia, Koma was a native of Botswana who felt that Seretse should publically denounce South Africa's racism. Seretse, however, insisted on neutral relationships with both Rhodesia and South Africa. Not only did many Botswanans work in these countries, but it was necessary for his landlocked homeland to depend on them for trade and for transportation to the rest of the world.

Meanwhile, some of the chiefs of the Batswana tribes were dismayed at their loss of prestige and influence under the new government. They felt the House of

The drought of the 1960s ruined Botswana's crops and killed many cattle. Threatened with famine, the people struggled through this long drought.

BOTSWANA INFORMATION SERVICES

Independence Day. Left: President Seretse and Lady Khama that night. Below: Khama addresses a crowd at the National Stadium that day.

PHOTOS ON THIS PAGE COURTESY OF BOTSWANA INFORMATION SERVICES

Chiefs should be equal in power to the Assembly, rather than merely an advisory body. The chiefs feared their long-held rights to determine who could use land in the tribal areas would be ended. Some of the chiefs helped form the Botswana National Union—similar to a political party—to push their views.

A NEW REPUBLIC

Under the British parliamentary form of government, the legislature is the strongest branch of government. Under the American republican form, the executive, judicial, and legislative branches all have equal power.

Seretse realized that his new nation would need a strong president to counteract the conservative factions of the legislature, including the House of Chiefs, whose members wanted to cling to the old ways of doing things. His government put forth plans for a new constitution combining the British and American types of government. It had both a strong legislature, modeled on the British system, and a strong president, modeled on the American system.

Early in 1966 the Legislative Assembly approved the new constitution, as did the British government. On September 30 of that year, the Republic of Botswana became the thirtieth African nation to receive full independence. The British Union Jack was lowered and the new flag of Botswana raised in its place. The flag displayed a light blue field, broken by a wide black stripe bordered on top and bottom by narrow white stripes.

Seretse Khama (grandson of the chief who had brought the Batswana tribes together and nephew of the regent-chief who had kept them together) was, at the age of forty-five, elected first president of Botswana by the National Assembly, as the new legislature was to be called. At his side was his wife, whose skin color had once forced him to renounce the chieftainship of his tribe. Now he was the elected leader of all the tribes—indeed, of all the people—of Botswana.

PATH TO THE FUTURE

In 1969 Seretse announced that his government finally had settled the long-standing question of the Tati Concession in northeastern Botswana, which had been under the control of South Africa since the Union was formed. For several million dollars, this district was bought back from South Africa, ending at last the disagreement over its ownership.

For many years black refugees fleeing South Africa and Rhodesia had entered Botswana, many of them settling there permanently. Others had gone to other parts of Africa, crossing the Zambezi River at the short border between Botswana and Zambia. At times, warning gunfire from either South West Africa or Rhodesia had made crossing by boat a dangerous escapade, but neither country had ever seriously attempted to stop this so-called "freedom ferry." Groups of people hoping to free Rhodesia from white rule were heading toward Rhodesia, attempting to enter Botswana from Zambia.

In 1969 Seretse announced that a loan from the United States of America would at last enable the building of a bridge between Botswana and Zambia. The bridge would not be so much a defiance of the white-ruled neighboring countries as it would be an indication of the friendship between the two black republics.

Under the constitution, the president and National Assembly are elected for five years, unless the president calls for elections before that term is up. Seretse called for new elections on October 18, 1969, almost a year ahead of schedule. This time only slightly more than half of the registered voters went to the polls, as compared with 75 percent some four years earlier. Perhaps this was an indication that the people were satisfied with Seretse's government and felt certain that his party would win again.

Seretse's Democratic Party did win, although it took only twenty-four seats in the Assembly. Three seats each went to Matante's People's Party and Koma's National Front, while Mpho's Independence Party won one seat.

The refusal of Seretse Khama to let Botswana take either the path of its white-racist neighbors or the path of black nationalistic nations elsewhere in Africa had once again been approved by the voters. At least for the foreseeable future, Botswana would follow its integrated, neutral plan toward peace and economic success —a path of its own choosing.

MICHAEL ROBERTS

The National Assembly Building, Gaborone.

THE GOVERNMENT OF BOTSWANA

Botswana's constitution provides for a government modeled on both the British and the American systems. Some legal experts think it follows the best parts of both and may even be better than either.

The president is both head of state, as in the United States, and head of government, as in Britain. He is named by the National Assembly, rather than elected by the people, and is always leader of the majority party in the Assembly. His term cannot exceed the five-year term of the Assembly.

With the assistance of other party leaders, the president chooses the vice-president and the Cabinet from the members of the Assembly. There is no specific number of Cabinet members, who are called ministers. In 1972 there were ministers of Development Planning and Finance; Home Affairs, Health, and Labor; Education; Works and Communications; Agriculture; Commerce, Industry, and Water Affairs; Local Government; and External Affairs—a total of eight ministers.

The Assembly is a single body, composed of thirty-six members. Thirty-one members are elected, one from each of the thirty-one election districts; four are appointed by members of the Assembly, and usually belong to the majority party in the Assembly. The attorney general is the last member of the Assembly; he may speak in the Assembly chamber, but he has no vote.

Though the president, also, may not vote in the Assembly, he may call it into session, speak before it, and dissolve it, calling for new elections at any time he feels the Assembly may not be backing him; thus, while Assembly members are elected to five-year terms, they may sit for a shorter period of time.

In a bow to Botswana's ancient customs of tribal leadership, the constitution calls for a House of Chiefs with twelve members. Eight members are the hereditary heads of the main Batswana tribes and four are elected by chiefs of minority tribes. Any legislation the Assembly considers regarding tribal affairs must be referred to, but not necessarily approved by, the House of Chiefs. The chiefs have lost their great hereditary power, and today sit only as an advisory body. They can, however, still run individually for election to the National Assembly.

The High Court of Botswana is headed by the chief justice, appointed by the president. Lesser judges are named by a special commission.

Since independence, local government has been divided into twelve councils, each of which is allowed to tax its residents. Nine councils represent districts and three represent individual towns (Gaborone, Lobatse, and Francistown).

Included in the constitution is a code of human rights forbidding racial discrimination.

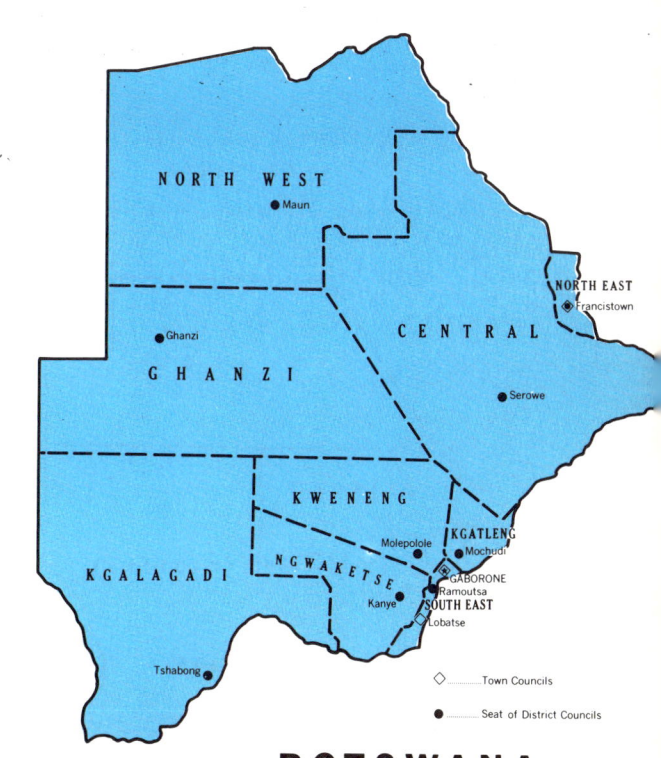

BOTSWANA COUNCILS

Botswana has no army or defense force. It has signed a pact with Britain for support in case military action is necessary.

EDUCATION

"Education is one of the most effective factors in the process of nation-building. Nations are, to a very large extent, built in the classroom." These words, spoken by President Seretse Khama in 1970, show the importance the young Republic of Botswana has placed on education.

Unlike many African lands, the protectorate of Bechuanaland received little help from the British or from church organizations in building schools. Most of the little money that was spent for education came from the tribal treasuries that were set up in 1938.

As late as 1970, only about one third of the people of Botswana could read and write in Setswana, the native language. About one fourth were literate in the English language. Though these figures seem low to Americans, they are generally high for emerging African nations.

The first secondary school was built by the Bamangwato under Tshekedi. Opened in 1947, it was called Moeng College (from the British idea of calling a second-

Botswana children learn to read and write in Setswana, the native language.

These girls take a break from their studies to play basketball.

ary school a college). With independence, a first priority was for new secondary schools. Within a few years, secondary school enrollment tripled, reaching about four thousand students in a dozen schools by 1970.

There are also an agricultural training college, a veterinary school, a training school for clerical and business students, and several teacher training schools.

Botswana has no university within its borders. Each year a few secondary school graduates are able to attend a university in England or the former Pope Pius XII College, later renamed the Joint University of Botswana, Lesotho, and Swaziland, located in Lesotho. Fewer than a dozen Botswana students attended this university in the early 1960s. By 1969 about 170 students were studying abroad, either privately or under government grants.

There are more than a hundred thousand children of primary school age in Botswana, but less than half of them attend school. There is not yet enough money to build needed schools and train needed teachers. Most primary schools are run and financed by the district and town councils, with some central government aid.

Since so few primary school graduates are able to continue their education, many pupils drop out before finishing eighth grade. As President Seretse indicated, the nation of Botswana will not grow until it has more classrooms.

53

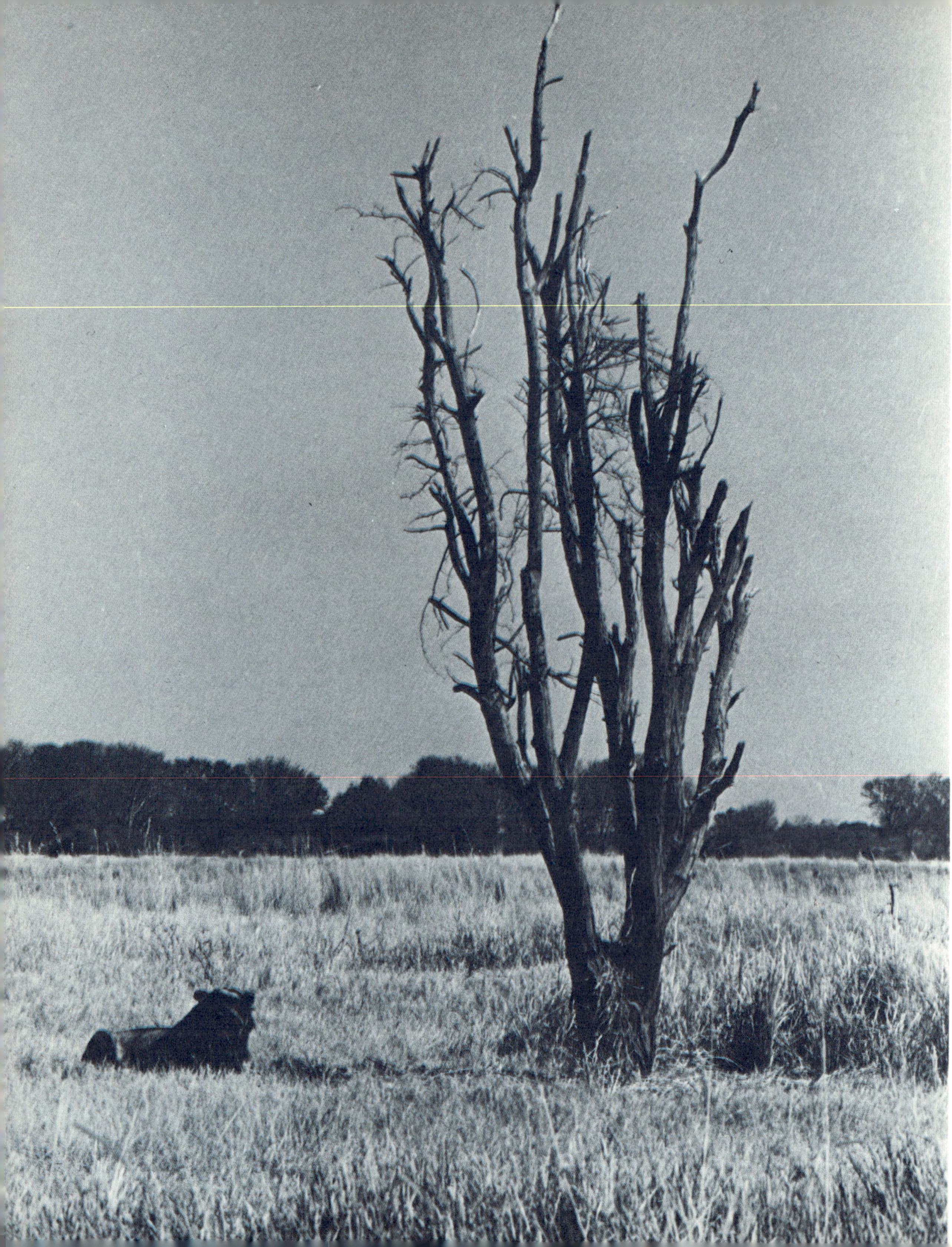

BOTSWANA INFORMATION SERVICES

Natural Treasures

LIVING THINGS

Compiling an accurate listing of every kind of animal in Botswana would be a staggering task. There would be hundreds—perhaps thousands—of kinds of wild animals, birds, and fish, and the list would probably include all of the species known throughout central and southern Africa.

White settlers and hunters have never entered Botswana in large numbers to trap and shoot the wildlife. Until the last fifty years or so, the total native population was small enough—less than a quarter of a million in an area almost as big as Texas—to allow the wildlife to thrive.

Today, as in the past, great portions of the land are unpopulated by man. Most of the human population is concentrated along the eastern border and in a few spots in the north. Elsewhere—in the Kalahari Desert and the Makarikari Salt Pans, in the Okavango Swamps and the Chobe Game Reserve—the wildlife is seldom bothered.

Elephants, black-maned lions, hippopotamuses, warthogs, leopards, zebras, and some rhinoceroses roam in the north. Inland, on the grassy desert that is not really a desert, are herds of buffalo, foxes, giraffes, and wildebeests.

Botswana has an amazing number of species of wild antelope, including the sable antelope, with its long, curving horns; the eland, the largest antelope of all, said to resemble an ox; the brown-gray kudu; the waterbuck and reedbuck, both named for their ability to swim across the reed-choked rivers of the swamps; the springbok, so called for its ability to spring into the air when running; the lechwe; the roan antelope, named for its color; the small

The lion is one of the many species of animal that can be seen in the bushland of Botswana.

There are hundreds—perhaps thousands—of kinds of wild animals in Botswana, including many species of antelope such as the red lechwe (left). Zebras (below) roam in the north. Giraffes (right) and buffalo (below right) are found on the grassy desert of central Botswana.

PHOTOS ON THESE PAGES
COURTESY OF BOTSWANA
INFORMATION SERVICES

red-brown impala with horns shaped like a lyre; the bushbuck of the Chobe region, sometimes called harnessed antelope because of the striped markings resembling a harness; and the small oribi.

The Kalahari Desert is said to be the last place on earth where one can see the nearly extinct gemsbok, or gemsbuck, whose long, straight horns help make it the most beautiful of the oryx type of antelope.

Although the number of crocodiles is diminishing, they can still be seen along the banks of the few Botswana rivers that flow year-round. There are also poisonous snakes, including puff adders and poison-spitting cobras.

The Chobe Game Reserve has begun to draw attention as "an ornithologist's paradise." Birds of every description can be seen, especially along the Chobe River, where hornbills, pelicans, shrikes, vultures, bustards, fish eagles, and other kinds of fish-eating species are plentiful.

On the Kalahari Desert are flightless ostriches, the largest birds in the world. Their huge eggs are considered delicacies by the Bushmen. A rare sight along the rivers is Stanley's Blue Crane, a beautiful, gray, long-legged wading bird.

The waters of the Chobe River and the Okavango River and Swamps are teeming with fish.

According to one fisheries expert, there are so many fish that millions could be caught each year and used for food without noticeably thinning the total supply.

The largest fish of Botswana is the barbel, a kind of carp that weighs as much as fifty pounds. Also found are the tiger fish, sometimes called the freshwater barracuda, which reaches twenty-two pounds, and the small Chobe bream, or tilapia.

MINERAL RESOURCES

When Europeans first explored and settled in southern Africa, they ignored the region now called Botswana. As far as they knew, it had none of the diamonds, gold, copper, and coal (and later, uranium) found in the neighboring territories. Gold was discovered in Botswana in 1866, but the mines did not produce great quantities of that much sought-after metal.

Not until the middle of the twentieth century were fantastic reserves of many valuable minerals finally discovered in Botswana. Thus far, few of these reserves have been tapped, and the republic's mineral wealth has yet to be accurately determined. One of these, a recently discovered diamond field, is said to be one of the largest and most valuable in the world. There are also enormous deposits of copper and nickel that, if properly mined, could make Botswana a very rich nation. Only recently has the government realized that the Makarikari Salt Pans could probably produce great annual quantities of salt, a most desired substance in southern Africa.

Small amounts of gold and silver still are mined. Other known minerals, most of

Though water is taken for granted in many parts of the world, Botswana's lack of it is a constant problem. River banks help during wet seasons.

them unexploited, are manganese, asbestos, iron, lead, kyanite, soft coal, and potash.

In many parts of the world, water is taken for granted, but in Botswana, it is one of the scarcest resources. Except in the swamplands to the north, where surface water is plentiful, adequate supplies for drinking can be obtained only by digging wells and boreholes. And in times of drought, some of these go dry, causing disaster to men and cattle alike.

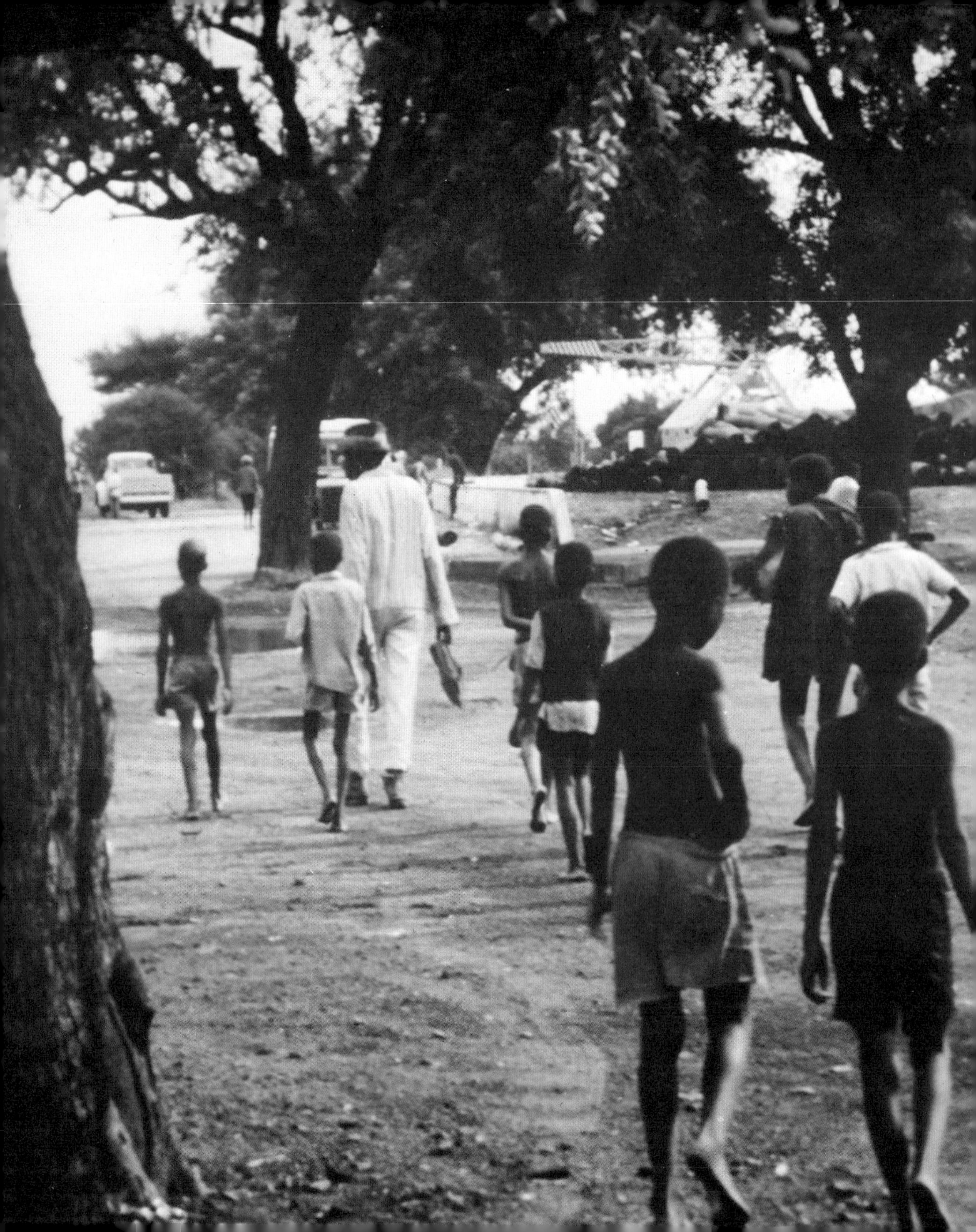

The People Live In Botswana

POPULATION

No accurate count was made of the number of people in Botswana until 1964. In that year a census showed the total population to be 543,105. Only eight years later, in 1972, the total had jumped to an estimated 624,000—a 15 percent increase! As in other African countries, this increase is partly due to better census techniques, as well as to an expected increase in population.

Not so many years ago, the population density was about 2.5 persons per square mile—one of the lowest not only in Africa, but in the world. Today, however, the density is approaching 3.0 and may soon exceed this number.

Unless the rate of population growth can be slowed, by the end of the century, there will be another half-million people in Botswana. The government faces great problems in employing and feeding such a large number in a nation that has little industry and relatively small acreage used for agriculture.

About 94 percent of the population are native Africans, or blacks, mainly members of the Batswana tribes. No one knows exactly how many Bushmen there are. Not even the census takers can count those wandering tribesmen accurately, but the estimated figure is ten thousand.

The European, or white, population is only about five thousand; it was never higher, even before independence. This

Most of Botswana's population is made up of native, black Africans. The rest of the population consists of Europeans, Eurafricans, Asians, and Bushmen.

ALLAN CARPENTER

The people at this village gathering are speaking Setswana.

small number of whites may be one reason why a white minority government did not evolve in Botswana as it did in South Africa, where the whites, although in the minority, total about four million. Most of Botswana's whites are descendants of those nineteenth-century British and Dutch settlers who moved into Botswana from South Africa. There are about five thousand persons of mixed racial backgrounds, often called Eurafricans, and less than one thousand Asians.

LANGUAGE AND RELIGION

All of the black people of central and southern Africa speak a variety of the language family called Bantu. In Botswana the language of the blacks is called Setswana; it is spoken as a first language by all of the tribes except the Bushmen.

The white settlers from Britain introduced the English language to the area. When Botswana received its independence, English was chosen as the official language, to facilitate trade and political dealings with the rest of the world.

The Dutch settlers from the Transvaal brought their Afrikaans language with them, and today many Afrikaaner words and phrases are commonly understood throughout Botswana.

The first whites in Botswana were missionaries, who sought to convert the natives to Christianity. Today only about 15 percent of the people are Christians, belonging to the Roman Catholic Church and various Protestant churches, including Anglican (Episcopalian), Presbyterian, Methodist, Pentecostal, and Dutch Reformed. Christian holidays such as Christmas and Easter, however, are celebrated nationwide. There are few Moslems, members of the Islamic faith.

Those natives who are not Christians tend to retain the beliefs common to all non-Islamic African tribes, known as *animism*. They believe that everything around them—trees, animals, and objects of all kinds—have "spirits" which must be treated with respect. The spirits of the dead, too, are feared, and must be respected and worshipped in ways dictated by age-old custom. These beliefs are an important part of African family life.

To some extent, the government is trying to prevent some of the cultural, if not religious, background of the Batswana people from disappearing. A marketing agency called Botswanacraft has been set up to sell native handcraft items outside the borders of the republic. This will not only keep alive the crafts of the past, it will also provide a much-needed source of revenue.

THE ETHNIC GROUPS

The people of the various ethnic groups, or tribes, of Botswana live peacefully today, just as they have for most of the years since they were united by Khama III. Although the chiefs no longer have their former powers, a sense of unity still holds the members together.

Botswanans today wear Western clothing and many live in Western-style houses. Some of them speak English and attend schools in England, but their heritage as members of a specific tribe still bands people together to care for the sick and elderly. They are inclined to vote for the candidate or party who would best serve their tribe as a whole, much as people in the United States choose the person who supports their own ethnic group.

President Seretse once reminded his people that they had achieved independence as a united people and urged them to remain united. "Unity does not simply consist in equality among tribes," he said. "It means that all Batswana must have a stake in Botswana's prosperity."

Under the British, each of the eight main tribes was given an area with a capital city. These lands were official designations of the areas that the tribes had occupied at the end of the 1800s. Members of one tribe could not farm or live in another tribe's land unless they received permission to do so from the other chief.

The eight areas totaled about 105,000 square miles, about half the country's total area. Except for the three blocks and the Tati Concession, the rest of Botswana was declared Crown Land—land retained by the government. This area was governed by the British without any native subcontrol and was made up mostly of desert area with very low population.

Bamangwato   The Bamangwato have produced the country's most prominent leaders. President Seretse Khama is a member of this tribe, as was his grandfather, Khama III. Today, the Bamangwato chief is Leapeetswe Khama. Not only are the Bamangwato the largest tribe in the republic, with about 40 percent of the population, but their lands cover more than 20 percent of the total area of Botswana.

The Bamangwato split away from the Bakwena not long before white men arrived in Botswana. Because of the strength of their chiefs, Bamangwato history is actually the history of the republic. Khama III was the main source of unity among the tribes in the 1800s. He supported the British, welcomed the missionaries, and brought a measure of education to the people.

Before 1900 tribal capitals were moved from time to time, depending on the supply of water and the whim of the chief. In 1902 the Bamangwato capital was moved from Palapye, along the railroad, to Serowe, about thirty miles to the west.

Bakwena   David Livingstone first settled with the Bakwena tribe, baptizing their chief, Sechele, a Christian. Presently, the Bakwena chief is Neale Sechele.

The Bakwena consider themselves the oldest tribe of the Batswana. From the Bakwena come both the Bamangwato and Bangwaketse tribes. Originally from the Transvaal region to the east, the Bakwena moved to their present location sometime in the 1700s. The Bakwena capital is at Molepolole, about thirty miles west of the railroad.

In olden times Bamangwato tribes moved often according to where water was available. Today village life still centers around water—at the water tap.

*A young Batawana boy returns
from visiting friends.
A boat like his is a commonly used
mode of transportation
in the Okavango Swamps.*

BOTSWANA INFORMATION SERVICES

Bangwaketse The Bangwaketse have a long history of hostilities, both with the Matabele of South Africa and within their own tribe. At one point they were forced out of their land by the Matabele; the Bangwaketse then fled to the South West Africa border. There have been disagreements over who should succeed to the chieftainship, causing opposing factions to split the tribe.

In 1889 Bathoen I became chief and brought a calming influence to the tribe. When he died, his wife, a daughter of the Bakwena Sechele, took power; she was succeeded by her daughter. Few other women have ever held the chieftainships of Batswana tribes. Seepapito IV is presently the chief; the tribal capital is at Kanye.

Batawana Seven of the eight main tribes live along the eastern border. The eighth, the Batawana, occupy the area known as Ngamiland in the northwest. Their area includes the Okavango Swamps.

The first Batawana chief was Tawana, whose father was chief of the Bamangwato. (Thus, the tribal name is a combination of two words—*Ba* meaning "men of," and *Tawana*.) Tawana and his half-brother argued over who was to succeed their father to the chieftainship of the

65

Some Bakgatla tribesmen of Mochudi sing a traditional song.

BOTSWANA INFORMATION SERVICES

Bamangwato. When the half-brother, Khama I, won, Tawana moved to the north and formed his own tribe, the Batawana. The current chief of this tribe is Letsholathebe.

The Batwana capital is at Maun, the only large town in Ngamiland. Other minor tribes living in the area are the Bayei, who preceded the Batawana there but were never able to overpower them; the Herero, who came from across the border in South West Africa when the Germans tried to destroy them there; and the Mbukushu, who live in the swamps.

The other major tribes have very small areas of tribal lands along the southeastern border of Botswana.

Bakgatla The Bakgatla of Botswana were driven out of the Transvaal by the Boers. They settled in what was then Bakwena land, with their capital at Mochudi. Their leader, Linchwe I, was a forceful man who refused to pay the Bakwena for the right to settle in their land. At one time Britain ordered him back across the border into the Transvaal, but he refused to go. In 1899 both the British and the Bakwena finally were forced to the realization that the Bakgatla had settled with the intention of staying, and their tribal area was then officially recognized.

Descendants of those Bakgatla who remained in the Transvaal still recognize the Botswana-Bakgatla chief as their own. As in many other parts of Africa, tribal borders here do not agree with political borders. Today the Bakgatla chief is M. Pilane.

Batlokwa Although most tribal names are derived from the founding chiefs, the Batlokwa were named for Tlokwe, a town in the Transvaal where they split off from a large tribe called the Bahurutse. In 1880 the chief of the Batlokwa, Gaberone, broke away from the main tribe. With a group of loyal followers, he moved to Moshaweng, a town that was in Bakwena tribal land in present-day Botswana.

The Bakwena later gave that particular land to the British South Africa Company. For many years, the Batlokwa paid the company a yearly rent for the privilege of remaining on their small seventy-square-mile plot. When Chief Gaberone died in 1932, Moshaweng was renamed Gaberones in his honor and the Batlokwa land officially became their tribal reserve. The block of land surrounding the reserve is known as the Gaberones Block.

Since 1966 the town, now spelled Gaborone, has been not only the capital of the Batlokwa but also the capital of the Republic of Botswana. The present chief of the Batlokwa is Kgosi Gaborone.

Bamalete Of the eight main tribes of Botswana, the Bamalete is the only one that is not of Batswana strain. The Bamalete originated to the east and are a Ndebele tribe. In 1875 they settled at Ramoutsa, their present capital, in what had been Bangwaketse land. The Bamalete lived as subjects of the Bangwaketse until 1885, when the British ceded this land to the British South Africa Company. When this cessation later was reversed, the Bamalete received the land as their own. Later, they purchased additional land from the Bangwaketse. Presently the chief of this tribe is Kelemogile Mokgosi, a regent.

Barolong The Barolong of Botswana are a small part of the large Barolong tribe of South Africa, with their capital and chief, Kebalepile Montshiwa, at Mafeking. They hold their native allegiance to a chief in another nation, though they recognize the Botswana government.

The Barolong are the only tribe of Batswana whose land was not controlled by the chief but was divided among the tribal members for farming purposes, with a minimum annual rent. The Barolong are the most productive farmers in the republic.

Minor Tribes There are many minor tribes who have never had official land reserves of their own. The Kaa, a division of the Barolong, live with the Bamangwato and Bakwena. The Kalaka, originally from Rhodesia, are not a Batswana people; they live in the Tati Concession. The Kgalagadi live on the edge of the desert; their name is actually another version of the word Kalahari. The Bahurutse, also of the Tati block, are part of a South African tribe.

THE BUSHMEN

The small, shy Bushmen, sometimes called Masarwa, of the Kalahari Desert are not related to any of the other tribes of Botswana. Their skin has a yellowish tinge and their faces have an Oriental look. According to one theory, they were the first tribe to settle in southern Africa, after being pushed southward by the black tribes, who were able to defeat them simply because the Bushmen were so small. The average height of a Bushmen is about four-and-one-half feet, though some are an inch or two more in height.

Survival is the one guiding purpose in the life of Bushmen—it drives out all other thoughts. Bushmen work for about three or four hours each day, catching or gathering such things as small animals, birds, insects, and snakes. Water is so difficult to find that they sometimes go without it for weeks, drinking instead the juices of animals they catch or the liquid of the wild tsama melon.

Since they must travel constantly in search of food and drink, Bushmen have no permanent villages. When they settle for a while at one spot, they make "homes" that are simple lean-tos constructed of a few branches. They have no leaders or chiefs. Each band—from the small eight- to twelve-member bands to the large ones of forty or fifty people—is guided by community necessity. Personal property is restricted to tools and weapons.

There are several tribes of Bushmen in Botswana; each has its own language. Their speech is unlike any other in the world. Along with consonants and vowels, the language has an unusual series of four or five clicks, made with the tongue against the roof of the mouth. Although Bushmen have no written language, some scholars have been able to represent the clicks by signs such as /, //, and !

Because of their nomadic ways, the number of Bushmen is difficult to tally in a census. There are probably about ten thousand of them in Botswana, but their number is declining. Some have been attracted by the modern ways of man and live on the edge of cattle ranches, wearing Western-style clothing. The Botswana government has dug boreholes for them in the Kalahari, and medical teams visit these watering spots to treat the Bushmen.

VILLAGES AND LAND LAWS

Traditionally, the Batswana have lived together in villages. This tradition started because the people wanted to be near water and because they could defend themselves more easily in groups.

Though some houses today are modern, square, cement structures roofed with tin, the old basic houses of the past are still the principal mode of shelter throughout Botswana. Most Batswana homes consist of several small, round houses placed together. These houses are encircled with a single, continuous round wall made of mud or earth. Atop each house is a cone-shaped roof made of *thatch,* a plant material similar to straw. The roof and wall do not meet, but are separated by an open space. The roof is supported by a framework on poles erected just outside the wall. A simple house has openings for the

Though some Batswana homes are modern, square, cement structures, most are small, round, thatched houses placed together. Above: An aerial view of a village near Shushong. Below: A typical village with a school and a kraal, or enclosure, for goats.

door and the windows; more sophisticated models have glass windows and a real door.

Around the home (or several huts) of a family is a low wall, three or four feet high, sometimes made from hedges but more often made of stone, earth, or mud. These walls follow beautiful, irregular curves, gently enclosing the huts of one family. Between the walls of different enclosures are narrow passageways used as lanes to get to other parts of the village. Sometimes all the walls of a village are decorated in similar style—with a painted line in some simple pattern.

From the air, a village presents an unusual abstract design with its cluster of coned roofs and serpentinely sculptured walls. Some critics have called Batswana villages a unique example of plastic (or molded) art designed to enclose space.

Until recently, the chief of a tribe controlled all the tribal land and allotted portions of it to individual members for farming. Except for the Barolong, individual members of a tribe could not possess land. In a large village, a farmer's plot might be a very long distance away from his home. All cattle were grazed on communal grazing land which, by custom, was never fenced. The young boys of the village watched the cattle to make sure they did not stray beyond the grazing area.

Today, with more and more young boys attending schools, there is no longer a large supply of cattle herders available. Fences are being built around tribal grazing compounds. Land tenure laws are slowly taking away the chiefs' power to distribute land. Instead, Land Boards have been set up in each tribe to rent, lease, or sell farming plots. For the first time, a man can feel that his plot of land is really his own, giving him much more incentive to use it properly. A move has been initiated to break down the large villages into smaller units so that a farmer's land will not be a long distance away from his home.

HEALTH

Botswana has always been prey to some of the diseases that occur in tropical Africa. With increased education and governmental expenditures, such diseases are slowly being brought under control.

Tuberculosis reaches almost epidemic proportions throughout the republic; it will take many years of treatment to get rid of it completely. A disease of the intestines, bilharzia, is caught from bathing in water containing the tiny snail that carries the disease.

Two diseases are found only in the wet northwestern swamps of Ngamiland. Both are carried by insects that do not thrive in the drier eastern lands where most of the people live. The anopheles mosquito, carrier of malaria, is the least dangerous of the two, since malaria can be prevented and cured by medicine.

The dreaded sleeping sickness is another story. It is carried by the tsetse fly, which injects the disease organism into the

Clinics such as this one help ease the load on the few hospitals in Botswana.

bloodstream when it bites men or cattle. The victim, man or cow, usually dies within a few weeks. In some parts of Ngamiland, herds of cattle have been destroyed and acres of land have been burned to prevent the fly from spreading. In the early 1960s entire villages were moved outside the fly belt.

Late in the 1960s the Botswana Tsetse Fly Control Department was organized. With aid from the World Health Organization, an insecticide spraying campaign began. Control points were set up on roads to check people and cattle passing from the fly belt. With the continued use of sprays, the tsetse fly may soon be stopped and the land it has scourged may once again be habitable.

By 1969 ten general hospitals and about one hundred health centers, clinics, and dispensaries had been set up in Botswana. Unfortunately, all of these are served by only thirty-four registered doctors and medical technicians. There is a great need for medical personnel in Botswana.

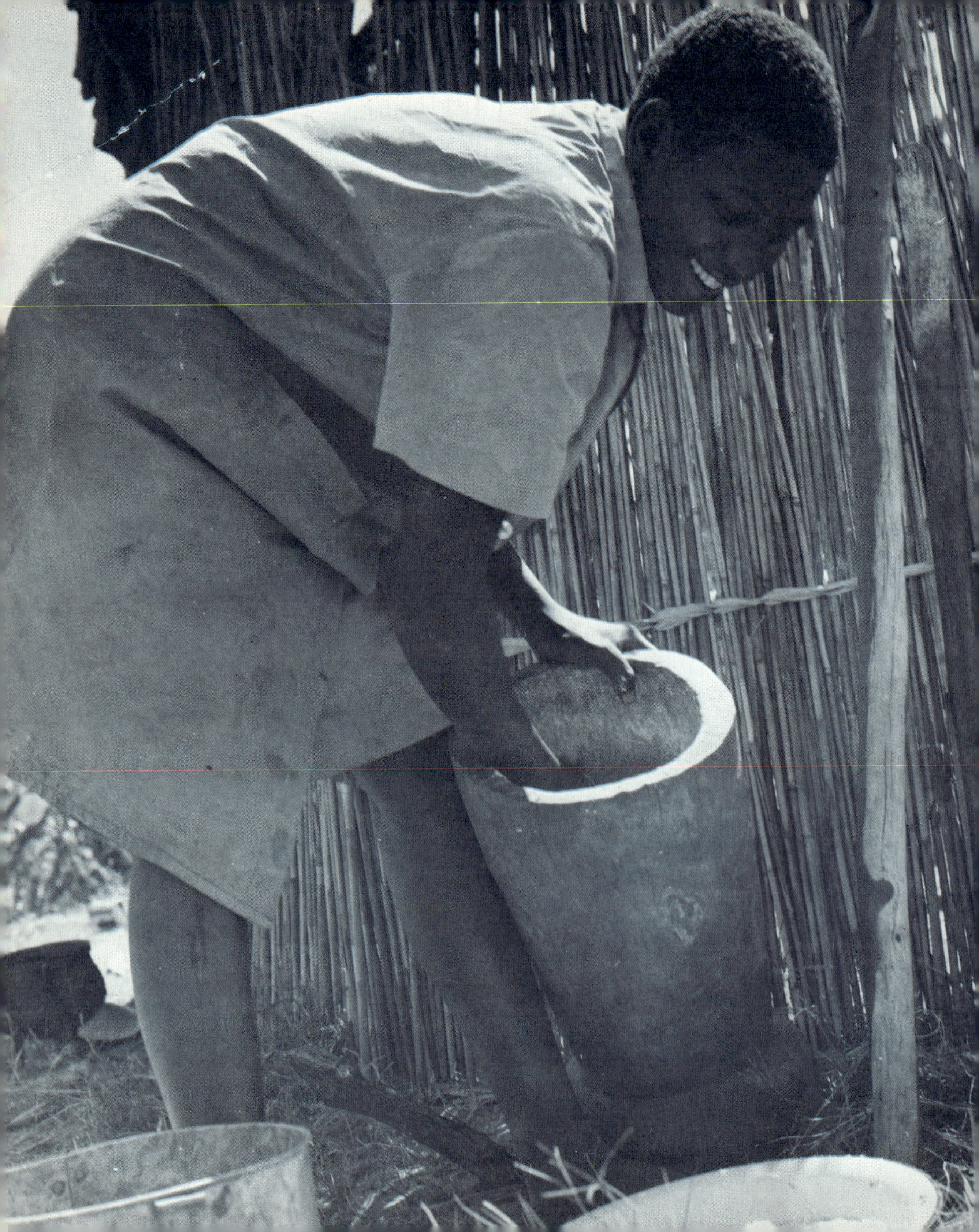

The People Work in Botswana

A NATION OF FARMERS

Botswana is basically a nation of farmers. Each man grows food for himself and his family on a small plot of land. Long-held custom as well as the whims of Nature have prevented the harvesting of large quantities of crops; there was no excess to be sold elsewhere in the republic or to be exported.

Only a small percentage—probably about 5 percent—of the land that could be cultivated is used for that purpose. The best farmland—the land along the eastern border—was claimed by white British and Dutch settlers in the late 1800s.

The main subsistence crops are sorghum, corn or maize, beans, and cow peas. Some farmers also raise chickens and pigs, not to be sold but to be eaten. A few crops, grown mainly by white farmers, are exported—cotton, citrus fruits, peanuts, soybeans, sunflowers, wheat, and even gladiolus bulbs.

Because native farmers use age-old methods, their land has a very low yield. Until recently, native farmers simply sowed their seeds by hand instead of planting them in rows. Plowing was done by hand or by ox-drawn plows.

Since independence, the government has set up Rural Training Centers to teach the natives how to increase their production. Native farmers are learning how to use fertilizers and pest- and weed-killing sprays. New strains of sorghum and corn better

One of Botswana's main crops is sorghum. This woman is preparing sorghum meal, the staple food of Botswana.

Cattle at Kgatleng Livestock Improvement Center. Cattle outnumber people in Botswana by more than two to one.

BOTSWANA INFORMATION SERVICES

able to withstand Botswana's dry climate have been introduced, as have methods of crop rotation.

Nature has always been the worst enemy of Botswana farmers. With so little rainfall, some farmers have felt that it was useless to devote much effort and time to growing crops that might not survive, and periods of drought have sometimes made it useless to plant any seed.

The government is planning a series of dams along the eastern border so that farmland can be irrigated during dry periods. A plan to construct a canal across some five hundred miles of desert, if carried out, would do much to improve agricultural prospects. The proposed canal would run from Sepopa, in the far northwest, around the swamps and through lakes Ngami and Xau, ending in Francistown and Serowe in the east. Waters from the Okavango River could then be pumped to where they are needed, rather than being lost in the swamps.

THE ONLY INDUSTRY

Cattle outnumber people in Botswana by more than two to one. They are more than just important to the republic—they are an economic necessity. The cattle industry is the only true industry in Botswana. Cattle and cattle by-products make up 90 percent of the republic's exports. More than 90 percent of the people own cattle or are employed on cattle ranches.

In the early 1960s the total national herd reached about 1.3 million head. Then came the long, tragic drought and thousands upon thousands of cattle died. Many farmers sold their cattle to avoid seeing them starve. By the late 1960s, the number of cattle was down to nine hundred thousand head.

With the end of the drought, cattle sales and exports dropped, as farmers rebuilt their herds. Today there are about 1.5 million head of cattle in the republic. Though there are some huge cattle ranches, most of them owned by whites, in general the herds are small. Every family owns a few head of cattle; they are as common in Botswana as telephones or television sets in the more industrialized parts of the world.

Because many of the cattle graze on unfenced communal grazing grounds, quality breeding is impossible. The grazing land is eventually destroyed from overuse. The government, however, is attempting to upgrade the quality of the livestock. The Livestock Improvement Center has organized demonstration ranches and advisory health centers to instruct farmers on modern methods of raising animals.

The cattle industry operates through the Botswana Meat Commission, formed by the government, the livestock producers, and the United Kingdom Commonwealth Development Corporation. This commission is said to be the largest meat export business in all of Africa.

The commission supervises the operation of the single large slaughterhouse in the republic, at Lobatse. Most of the cattle sold for export pass through Lobatse, except for a small percentage raised in Ngamiland. These cattle are sold and slaughtered in nearby Rhodesia.

Subsidiary products of the cattle industry are canned meats and extracts, hides and skins, bone meal, leather, soap, and dairy products. Except for small beer, liquor, and clothing plants, there are no other manufacturing concerns in Botswana. New factories are planned, however, that will be supported by the government. All other consumer goods are imported, mostly from South Africa and Rhodesia.

A DAZZLING PROMISE

As the decade of the 1970s opened, Botswana had exciting news of possible mineral wealth that could soon grow into a large industry. If mineral reserves are as large as recent exploration indicates, many millions of dollars will soon be invested in mining. The promise of income and employment is dazzling to a poor, young republic that has made what living it can on top of the ground, rather than under it.

Small quantities of gold, silver, manganese, and kyanite have been mined in Botswana from time to time. An asbestos mine has been in operation near the town of Kanye for more than twenty years. Not until the late 1950s, however, did a firm begin to explore for diamonds, which are found so plentifully across the border in South Africa.

In 1969 De Beers, the large diamond firm of South Africa, announced a great diamond find south of the Makarikari Salt Pans. Mining was scheduled to start in 1971 near the town of Orapa, in the mouth of an ancient, inactive volcano. The diamond site, which covers almost three hundred acres, is said to be one of the largest in the world.

Two years earlier, in 1967, the Botswana Roan Selection Trust announced it had discovered a huge copper and nickel field at Pickwe, a few miles from Serowe. An estimated thirty to forty million tons of the two metals are said to lie buried there.

Both the new diamond and copper-nickel fields are in Bamangwato tribal lands, as are newly discovered soft coal fields. The Bamangwato, however, will not be the only Batswana to profit, by granting concessions to mining companies. In 1969 the government, with Bamangwato agreement, took over the mineral rights to the new finds. Thus, all of Botswana will gain enormously should the republic become a center of mining activity.

The mines will create new job opportunities, raising the employment rate. Already a new road is being built from Francistown to Orapa. Small subsidiary industries are bound to spring up around the mines. Since large amounts of water are needed in diamond mining, the find at Orapa may cause the proposed cross-country canal from the Okavango River to become more than just a dream.

As President Seretse stated, "The exploitation of these mineral resources... will have freed us of the need for financial assistance from foreign sources."

WILDLIFE DRAWING CARD

Another possible source of income for Botswana is tourism. Today tourists traveling in southern Africa visit sites near Botswana's borders, but few tourists cross over into the republic.

A few miles from the spot where the Chobe and Zambezi rivers meet is Victoria Falls, on the Zambia-Rhodesia border; it is one of the most spectacular and most often-visited sites on the continent. Just across the southern border with South Africa is a national park, a favorite of visitors to that nation. Botswana must promote its own attractions to draw these nearby tourists to the republic.

Although Botswana has no single great attraction like Victoria Falls, its abundant wild animal life could be a tremendous drawing card. In 1962 a United Nations ecological team stated that "Botswana contains the largest concentration of plains game in Africa today."

The Chobe River is a natural magnet for sports fishermen, and the Chobe Game Reserve, just an hour and a half from Victoria Falls, could someday soon be famed

Only recently were huge diamond fields and copper/nickel fields discovered in Botswana. Above: Miners after an underground shift at the Kgwakgwe mine in Kanye. Right: A plant at the Selebi-Pickwe diamond mine. Below: A miner at the Selebi-Pickwe copper/nickel mine waits inside for the call to start work.

PHOTOS ON THIS PAGE COURTESY OF BOTSWANA INFORMATION SERVICES

The donkey cart, a common means of transportation among the Batswana.

SANDY GRANT

as one of the best wildlife parks in the world. Hunting and photography safaris already are conducted around the reserve, but as yet they have not been well publicized. The Moremi Wildlife Reserve, north of Maun, was opened by the Batawana tribe in 1962.

Before tourists will come in large numbers, new hotels, roads, and airfields must be built. All of these have been planned. Many travelers will avoid Ngamiland until all traces of malaria and sleeping sickness are gone. Meanwhile, tourists in Botswana have an exciting, if rough and uncomfortable, experience in store for them.

TRANSPORTATION AND COMMUNICATION

Improved transportation would not only help the tourist industry, but it would be a boon to all the people of Botswana. Today it is nearly impossible to reach some parts of the republic quickly and easily.

The railroad built by Cecil Rhodes, still the only railroad in Botswana, follows the route of the old British missionary trail used by early settlers to travel from Cape Town, South Africa, to what is now Rhodesia. It provides slow but reliable connections with Pretoria and Johannesburg in South Africa and with Rhodesia and other countries in east-central Africa.

The line travels 394 miles in crossing Botswana, beginning at Ramathlabama in the south. After passing through some of the main towns of the republic, including Lobatse, Gaborone, and Francistown, it crosses the northern border at the Ramaquabane River.

At one time in the last century, a railroad was planned from Francistown to Maun, but plans never advanced farther than a partial survey. Botswana has no railroad or improved road connections with South West Africa.

Although there are about five thousand miles of roads, only forty miles are paved with asphalt. The rest are gravel and dirt roads, and some can be used only by four-wheel-drive vehicles in rainy weather.

The main north-south road, sometimes called the Border Road, runs parallel to the entire line of the railroad. The two main east-west roads start at Francistown. One road skirts the northern edge of the Makarikari Salt Pans, ending at Maun; the other is the new road to the diamond field at Orapa.

Shorter east-west roads run from Palapye to Serowe, from Lobatse to Kanye, and from Gaborone to Molepolole. There is what seems to be an endless road from Kanye across the desert to Ghanzi, but it is a sand track open only to four-wheel-drive vehicles. Similar tracks cross other less-populated areas of Botswana.

The government has plans for a road from the town of Nata, on the Francistown-Maun road, north to Kazungula, at the Zambian border. This road would be of great economic importance, as it would allow easy shipment of exports to Zambia and other nations to the north.

In Botswana traffic moves on the left side of the road, in the British fashion.

Border Road is a dirt and gravel road that runs parallel to the railroad.

Both gasoline and automobiles are expensive. As late as 1968 there were only 5,101 registered vehicles, of which fewer than 3,000 were private cars.

The national airline, called Botswana National Airways, connects the main towns of the republic. It also makes several round trips each week to Lusaka in Zambia and to Johannesburg in South Africa. None of the dozen or so airstrips in Botswana are big enough to handle large jet planes.

There are no television broadcasting stations in Botswana, nor are any newspapers published. Though some South African newspapers are sold, the best way to keep up with the news is through broadcasts on the national radio station, Radio Botswana. Founded at about the time of independence, the station broadcasts in both English and Setswana. Besides news and entertainment, it has educational and agricultural programs on both the AM band and shortwave stations.

Telephone and telegraph service is available in both large and small towns, but these services are usually available only during business hours in small towns.

EMPLOYED AND EMPLOYABLE

When a young man reaches adulthood in Botswana, naturally he wants to find a job. Since there is so little industry and manufacturing, few jobs are available. Only about seventy thousand persons receive wages for employment, though the potential work force is more than twice that number.

More than half of the seventy thousand employed work outside of Botswana. There is a century-old tradition of migrant labor, stretching back to the 1870s when workers were first recruited to work the South African mines. Today it is as common for a young Batswana man to sign up for work in South Africa as a miner as it is for young men elsewhere in the world to sign up for military service.

Migrant workers return to Botswana only for short periods of time during their employment, which may last anywhere from a year or two to twenty years or more. Most of these men work from their late teens to their middle or late twenties, when they return home, marry, and become farmers if they are unable to find

An airplane at the airport in Gaborone. This airline connects the main towns of the republic.

BOTSWANA INFORMATION SERVICES

any other employment. Few of them stay on in South Africa permanently because of the apartheid laws there.

The largest employer in Botswana is the government. It offers jobs in civil service, police work, medicine, and teaching. Other workers are employed by the Lobatse slaughterhouse and by large cattle ranches and farms.

The rest of the employable men must make do with their farmland and a few head of cattle. In 1970 the per capita income (total national income divided by total population) was only $94. If mining develops into a thriving industry, it will offer many new jobs and help to raise the standard of living.

NEIGHBORLY TRADE

Botswana's economy has been growing at the rate of 15 percent a year, one of the fastest rates in the world. Despite its differences with the white-supremist government of Rhodesia and the apartheid rule of South Africa, Botswana is forced by geographical circumstances to carry on most of its trade with those two nations.

Since it manufactures so few items, Botswana consistently shows a negative balance of trade; that is, it imports much more than it exports. In 1968, for example, imports totaled $28 million, while exports came to only $10.5 million. About two thirds of the imports came from South Africa and one third of the exports went to that country.

Cattle, meat, and meat by-products make up about 85 percent of the exports; about 6 percent are minerals and agricultural crops; 9 percent is migrant labor. Migrant wages, sent back to Botswana, bring between $1 million and $2 million a year into the republic.

Besides foods and grains, the major imports are manufactured items of every conceivable kind, from cars and gasoline to clothes and shoes.

One of the government's largest sources of income is the revenue collected on imports. Along with Swaziland, Lesotho, and South Africa, Botswana belongs to the South African Customs Union. No customs duties are collected on items traded among the four republics.

South Africa levies and collects customs on all items traded between each of these republics and the rest of the world. Each of the three smaller nations gets a percentage of the total customs duties that South Africa collects each year. In 1969 a new agreement brought the three countries' share to 42 percent of all collected customs.

All three of the small republics also use the South African monetary unit, the *rand*. One rand is worth about $1.40 in United States currency. Botswana has no large national banks of its own, but there are about forty branches of large British banks. Individuals may also keep savings accounts in Post Office Savings Bank agencies. The National Development Bank, run by the government, is designed to aid small businesses with loans.

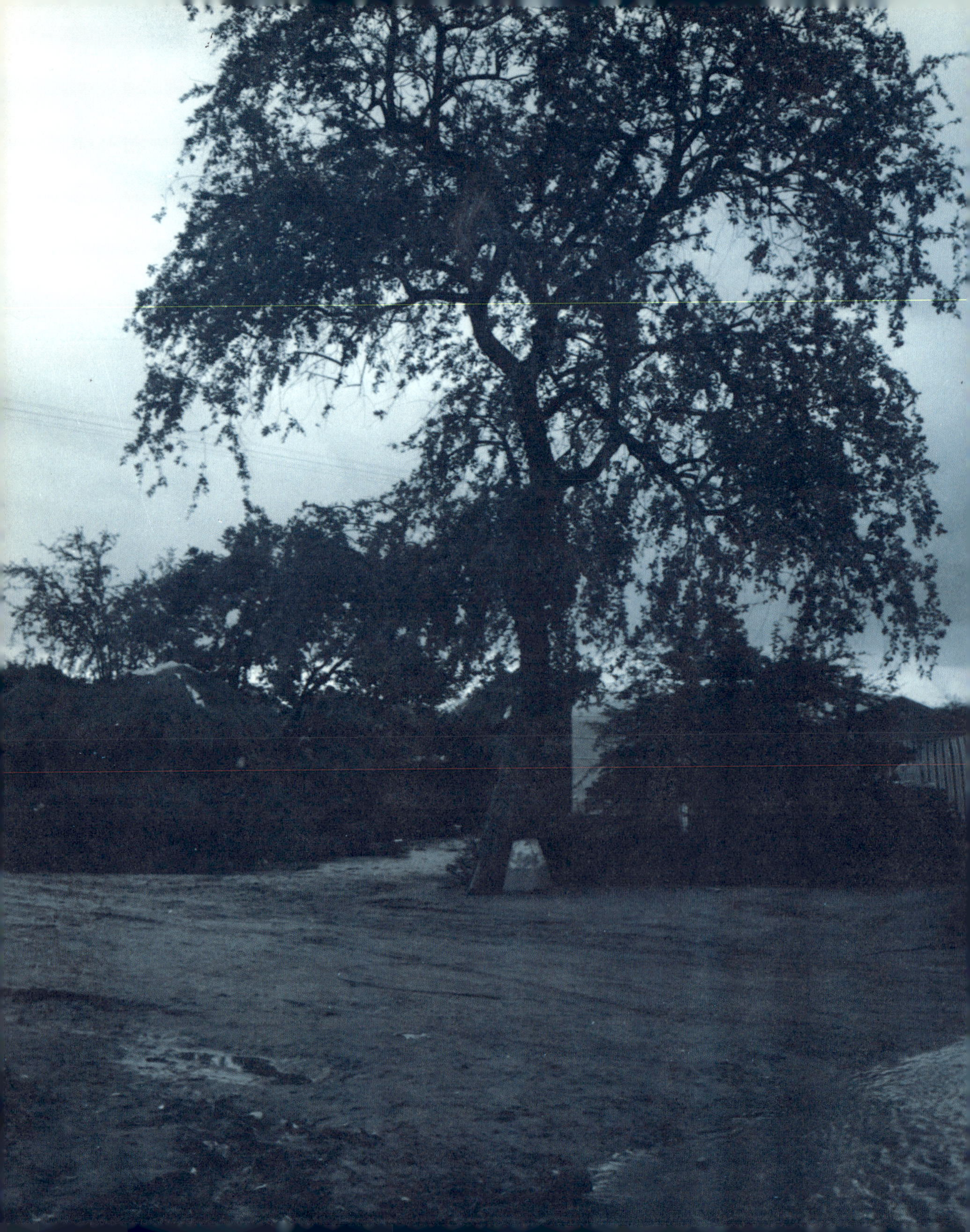

Enchantment of Botswana

ALONG THE RAILROAD

Eighty percent of the population of Botswana lives along the eastern edge of the country, near the railroad. They live in small towns and villages; the largest city in the republic has a population of less than forty thousand. A few of the towns have English or Afrikaaner names such as Martin's Drift and Dead Mule or Schoongezicht, but most carry names in the native Setswana tongue.

Moving north from the place where the railroad crosses into Botswana from South Africa, the first large town is Lobatse. Settled in a shallow valley between low hills, Lobatse is the business and industrial "capital" of Botswana, for it is the site of the republic's large slaughterhouse. About one thousand head of cattle a day are killed humanely and processed in the slaughterhouse. There is a cannery where some of the meat is packed and a soap factory that utilizes some of the waste fat from the cattle.

In Lobatse is a courthouse where the Legislative Council met from 1960 to 1965. This was before the capital city was moved from Mafeking, South Africa, to Gaborone, because the council did not desire to meet outside the borders of its territory. One of the most modern hotels in the republic, the Cumberland, is also in Lobatse.

The two largest towns in Botswana, Kanye and Serowe, are not located along the railroad. Kanye, about twenty-five miles northwest of Lobatse, is both the

As people flock to Gaborone, tents and trailors invade the old villages of thatched huts.
MICHAEL ROBERTS

tribal capital of the Bangwaketse and the capital of the Kgwaketse district council. With a hospital and an excellent secondary school, it is one of the more modern towns in the republic.

THE NEW CAPITAL

Until 1965, what is now the capital city of Botswana was a sleepy town, originally called Moshaweng. It had a few stores, a post office, a garage, and a small hotel, all built near the railroad station. About three miles from the station was the government camp or village, with another post office, schools, a jail, and government offices.

When Chief Gaberone of the Batlokwa died in 1932, Moshaweng was renamed Gaberones in his honor. Later the spelling was changed to Gaborone.

When Gaborone was chosen to be the capital, a neat and modern town was laid out in the open space between the railroad station and the government camp. At the center of the new section are government and commercial buildings. Surrounding this, within a short walk, is the residential area.

The new buildings of Gaborone were designed in modern architectural style, although none is taller than three stories. There is a gleaming new structure in which the National Assembly meets, a new post office, a telephone building, a police station, several banks, schools, and a hospital. Plans are under way to pave all the roads in the new section of town.

One reason Gaborone was chosen as the capital was its fairly consistent supply of water from the Notwani River. Though the Notwani is often dry (like most of Botswana's rivers), the dam has long provided water for the town. Another large dam has also been built. It has a seven-mile-long reservoir walled in by piled-up earth, where people can fish and sail.

Governmental employees and the residents of Gaborone spend much of their leisure time at sports. A golf course, tennis courts, a swimming pool, and other sports facilities are available, many under the auspices of the Gaborone Sports Club. Films are shown in Gaborone at the movie theater, one of the few in Botswana.

The National Museum and Art Gallery opened in 1968. Its exhibits attempt to give a compact cultural history of Botswana. Its botanical garden has examples of the interesting plant life of the republic. In the year after independence, the National Archives and Archives Library was founded, with documents giving an unbroken picture of tribal and governmental history. The National Library Service, with a local library for Gaborone residents, is the first of a planned nationwide network of public libraries.

NORTH TO THE BORDER

Thirty miles east of Gaborone is the third largest town in Botswana, Molepolole, the tribal capital of the Bakwena.

The arrival of the Sunday afternoon passenger train from Capetown is an important social event for many Batswana.

MICHAEL ROBERTS

The bicycle is becoming an increasingly popular mode of transportation in Gaborone.

ALLAN CARPENTER

A modern shopping center in the middle of Gaborone will soon be completed and landscaped.

MICHAEL ROBERTS

This is the region where David Livingstone lived with the natives. He is still remembered and admired there, and Molepolole remains a center of London Missionary Society activities.

About 120 miles north of the capital along the railroad is the town of Mahalapye, the nearest rail stop for the farms in the Tuli block to the east. Fifty miles farther north is Palapye, where a road heads east to the town of Serowe, the capital of the Bamangwato. Serowe is not as well laid out as is new Gaborone, and it is a confusing mixture of new, modern houses and groups of native villages. Serowe sets an example for all the towns of Botswana, with its new schools and its large hotel.

The last large town on the railroad is Francistown, which is both a town council city and a district council capital, as well as the largest town in the Tati Concession.

Francistown has one main street, running along the railroad, faced with the main shops and houses and three hotels. It is the last stopping-off point on the north-south road for refugees from South Africa who are fleeing to Zambia. Francistown is also a center for the hiring of workers for South African mines.

Around the town—in fact, throughout the Tati Concession—are low stone ruins

In the Makarikari, a safari heads toward a baobab tree.

thought to date from the 1700s or earlier. They are probably the remains of walls built as protection around early native villages. Paintings of animals made by early inhabitants of what is now Botswana are found on rock walls near Francistown. As yet, few of the ruins or paintings have been studied by experts.

CHOBE GAME RESERVE

At the northernmost point of Botswana, nine miles from the river-border with Zambia, is the town of Kasane. It lies only an hour and a half by road from Victoria Falls, the great tourist attraction on the boundary between Zambia and Rhodesia.

Kasane is the northern entrance to the Chobe Game Reserve. It has a modern tourist hotel and a tourist camp providing electricity, parking sites, and running water. Eleven miles away, on the banks of the Chobe River, is Serondellas Camp, where powerboats and guides can be hired.

At present there are about fifty miles of good roads and tracks in the forty-five hundred square miles of the game reserve. Four-wheel-drive vehicles are needed to explore the more distant parts of the park. Signs announce a speed limit of twenty miles per hour, and the game warden requests visitors to "please observe this limit—there are many hundreds of elephant and buffalo within an hour's drive of Kasane."

For those on photography safaris, camouflaged hiding spots have been built at permanent waterholes, and near Kasane is a hiding place built in a tree for hotel guests who wish to take pictures. Tourists desiring luxurious surroundings can stay at the hotel and use its facilities; those inclined to rough it may use their own cars or camping trailers at the camping sites.

Visitors who wish to fish or travel by boat on the Chobe River can do so anywhere, but fishing from the riverbank is restricted to certain areas. It seems that unrestricted fishermen sometimes pick spots that are favorite drinking places of elephants!

The Chobe Game Reserve is open the year round. The greatest number of game can be seen in the dry season, when animals congregate at waterholes that are filled year-round. In the wet season, though, the scenery is said to be at its most beautiful, and even then non-migratory animals such as elephants can be seen.

NGAMILAND AND GHANZI

South from Kasane through the Chobe Game Reserve is a road to Francistown. At the town of Nata a branch of this soon-to-be-improved road heads to the tribal lands of the Batawana, sometimes called Ngamiland. Here are the mysterious Okavango Swamps, with all their intriguing wildlife.

At the southeastern edge of the swamps is the town of Maun, capital of both the

Batawana tribe and the North West district council. The Batawana actually are a minority of the total population of the region, being outnumbered by other small tribes. Maun, with a total population of ten thousand, has fewer than a hundred white residents, but there is no racial segregation in this town.

South of Maun and Lake Ngami the swampland turns to desert. Along the border with South West Africa is the district called Ghanzi with its capital of the same name. Ghanzi is even more isolated from the rest of the world than is the Chobe Game Reserve. To get to eastern Botswana from Ghanzi, one must either drive the northerly route to Maun and then head east past the Salt Pans to Francistown, or else, throwing caution and comfort to the winds, drive on the sandy track across the Kalahari to Kanye.

The town of Ghanzi, however isolated, is a welcome sight to the adventurous traveler. There are a few shops, a hotel, a post office, a church, and a school. Most of the white people of the Ghanzi district are descendants of Boers who came from the Transvaal in the 1890s. They were given farmlands, but soon discovered that the rainfall was too sparse to allow for growing crops. They turned to raising cattle instead.

Living at Ghanzi is an expensive proposition. All food and supplies must be trucked in. Sending cattle for slaughter to Lobatse means a five-hundred-mile trip across the desert. There are plans to open a small slaughterhouse in Ghanzi itself.

KALAHARI'S LOST RUINS

Heading south from Ghanzi, over the long stretches of the Kalahari Desert, one encounters few people and fewer villages. The empty lengths of sand and grass and brush are broken every so often by a borehole where water is available. There are only two towns of importance in the Kalahari Desert—Tshane, about halfway to the southern border with South Africa, and Tshabong, only a few miles from the border.

In the far southern reaches of the desert are sand dunes. A very sensible means of transportation in that part of the desert is the camel. Since camels are not native to that part of Africa, they must be brought thousands of miles from northern Africa.

The scattered villages in the Kalahari are built around the boreholes. The people raise cattle and live very simply. Without readily available water, the only way to maintain life is to use the hunting and gathering techniques of the Bushmen. Should a borehole go dry, the people must move to some other location. Life on the desert is a meager, difficult existence.

It is not surprising that a romantic legend has sprung up about the Kalahari. In 1886 an American explorer told of finding the ruins of what seemed to be a city in the southern Kalahari. He described mortared walls built of flat stones and a sand-covered stone walkway shaped like a cross, at the center of which was the base of some type of altar or monument.

Ever since, others have been searching for this "Lost City of the Kalahari." From time to time, in some remote spot, a natural outcropping of rock resembling the American's description has been found, but such natural phenomena have no stones bound with mortar.

If the city did exist, why was it built in the middle of a desert? Where did the stones to build it come from? Who lived there? What finally happened to those people? No clues to these mysteries have yet been found, but adventurous explorers still roam the desert, hoping to rediscover the city's ruins.

The bleak Kalahari and its legends are typical of the enchantment of Botswana. In this land of desert and swamps, no one really knows what happened before two centuries ago. In its short history, Botswana has seen native wars followed by long years of peace, and long years of white domination followed by native black independence. The years before 1800 are still a mystery, awaiting further study by archaeologists and anthropologists.

It is said that Botswana is moving "from a dreamy colonial backwater to become a developing country in the real sense." The promise of mineral wealth, of trapped swamp waters waiting to be used for irrigation, and of empty land waiting to blossom with crops all spell a bright future. The people of Botswana are not looking to the past. They are eager for tomorrow.

In a developing country with a scarcity of water, dam building is essential.

Handy Reference Section

INSTANT FACTS

Political:
Official Name—Republic of Botswana
Capital—Gaborone
Form of Government—Republic
Monetary Unit—South African rand
Official Language—English
Religions—Animist, Roman Catholic, Moslem, Protestant
Flag—Light blue field with black, horizontal band at center that is edged with narrow, white stripes

Geographical:
Area—220,000 square miles (estimate)
Highest Point—about 5,000 feet
Mean Altitude—3,300 feet
Greatest Width (east to west)—600 miles
Greatest Length (north to south)—550 miles

POPULATION

Total Population—624,000 (1972 estimate)
Population Density—2.8 persons per square mile
Population Profile—94% black; others are whites, mixed, Asians, Bushmen
Literacy Rates—33% in Setswana; 25% in English
Per Capita Income—$94 (1969)

PRINCIPAL CITIES

Serowe	37,000
Kanye	37,000
Molepolole	32,000
Gaborone	20,000
Mochudi	20,000
Francistown	15,000
Ghanzi	10,000
Lobatse	10,000

GOVERNMENT DIVISIONS

Town Councils:
Gaborone
Lobatse
Francistown

District Councils:
North West (Maun)
North East (Francistown)
Central (Serowe)
Kgatleng (Mochudi)
Kweneng (Molepolole)
South East (Ramoutsa)
Ngwaketse (Kanye)
Kgalagadi (Tshabong)
Ghanzi (Ghanzi)

HOLIDAYS

May 24—President's Day
June 8—Commonwealth Day
September 30—Independence Day (Botswana Day)
Christian holidays such as Easter and Christmas

PRONUNCIATION NOTE

Batswana (Bahts-wan-a)—Major tribal group; used to refer to the people of Botswana
Bechuanaland (Betch-wan-a-land)—British name for protectorate
Botswana (Bahts-wan-a)—Name given to Bechuanaland after independence in 1966

YOU HAVE A DATE WITH HISTORY

1820—Robert Moffat of London Missionary Society founds village at Kuruman
1840—British control southern Africa; Dutch settle in Transvaal
1841—David Livingstone begins long stay in Bechuanaland as missionary-explorer
1866—Gold discovered in Tati; Boers take over region
1870s—Khama III becomes chief of Bamangwato
1881—Pretoria Convention sets Limpopo River border
1884—London Convention redefines border; British attack Boers at Mafeking
1885—British claim Bechuanaland Protectorate and British Bechuanaland
1889—British South Africa Company receives mining rights
1895—Khama III and two other chiefs protest exploitation by British South Africa Company to Queen Victoria; British settlers raid Boers in Johannesburg
1899—Boer War begins in Transvaal
1910—British form Union of South Africa
1920—Native and European (white) Advisory Councils organized
1923—Great Chief Khama III dies
1933—Pim Report on Bechuanaland
1934—Native proclamations define powers of chiefs
1936—Charles Arden-Clarke named British commissioner
1938—Arden-Clarke sets up tribal treasuries
1943—New native proclamations
1947—Moeng College, first secondary school, opens
1948—Seretse Khama marries Ruth Williams, a white woman, in London
1951—Joint Advisory Council replaces advisory councils of 1920
1952—Tshekedi returns to Bamangwato tribal lands from exile
1956—Seretse's exile revoked, returns to Bechuanaland
1959—Tshekedi Khama dies
1960—Legislative and executive councils formed; first constitution planned; first political party formed
1961—Republic of South Africa proclaimed
1962—Seretse organizes Democratic Party; first demands for independence
1960s—Five-year drought; world relief groups send aid
1963—British plan internal self-rule for Bechuanaland; five-year economic plan announced
1964—Racial segregation banned; census sets population at 543,105
1965—Capital moved to Gaborone; first elections; Seretse named prime minister; first Legislative Assembly meets
1966—Republic of Botswana receives independence from Great Britain; Seretse becomes first president
1967—Copper-nickel deposits discovered at Pickwe
1969—Seretse calls and wins election; diamond find at Orapa; new customs agreement with South Africa
1972—Population shows 15 percent increase over previous eight years

Index

African Council, 35
Afrikaans language, 62
Agriculture, 73
Angola, 11, 12
Animals, 55-58
Animism, 63
Apartheid laws, South Africa, 20, 39
Arden-Clarke, Charles, 36
Area, 11
Asians, 62

Bahurutse, 67
Bakgatla, 28, 66
Bakwena, 8, 28, 30, 40, 41, 64, 66, 67, 84
Bamalete, 28, 67
Bamangwato, 8, 9, 28, 31, 36, 39, 40, 41, 42, 52, 64, 65, 66, 67, 76, 86
Bangwaketse, 8, 9, 28, 64, 65, 67, 84

Bangwato (Bamangwato), 28
Barolong, 28, 67
Basutoland, 35, 41
Batawana, 28, 65, 66, 78, 87, 88
Bathoen (chief), 8, 9, 65
Batlokwa, 28, 67, 84
Batswana, 27, 28, 31, 35
Bayei, 66
Bechuanaland Democratic Party, 42, 46, 50
Bechuanaland People's Party, 42, 46, 50
Bechuanaland Protectorate, 7-9, 12, 32, 34
Birds, 58
Boers, 7, 8, 9, 28, 30, 31, 32, 34, 88
Boer War, 34
Border Road, 79
Boreholes, 15
Botletle River, 12, 14
Botswana Meat Commission, 75

Botswana National Airways, 80
Botswana National Front, 47, 50
Botswana National Union, 49
Botswana Protectorate, 46
Botswana Roan Selection Trust, 76
Boundaries, 11
British Bechuanaland, 32
British South Africa Company, 8, 9, 32, 34, 67
Bushmen, 12, 16, 23-25, 27, 45, 61, 62, 67, 68

Cabinet, 51
Cape Colony, 7, 8, 30, 32
Cape of Good Hope, 28
Capital cities, 34, 45
Caprivi Strip, 11, 12
Cattle, 19, 20, 70, 71, 74, 75
Census, 1964, 45, 61

Chiefs, House of, 44, 47, 49, 51
Chobe Game Reserve, 21, 55, 58, 76, 87
Chobe River, 11, 15, 21, 58, 76, 87
Churchill, Sir Winston, 41
Climate, 16, 17
Commissioners, British, 35, 36, 44
Communications, 80
Constitutions, 41, 44, 49, 50
Copper, 58, 76
Councils of Botswana, 11, 51
Courts, 51
Crocodile (Limpopo) River, 15
Crops, 73
Crown Lands, 34, 63
Customs Union, 81

Dams, 39, 74, 84, 89
De Beers, 76

92

Democratic Party, 42, 46, 50
Diamonds, 58, 76
Droughts, 17, 47, 74, 75
Dutch Boers, 7, 8, 9, 28, 30, 31, 32, 34, 88

Economy, 81
Education, 20, 21-23, 37, 52, 53
Employment, 80
Ethnic groups, 61
Eurafricans, 62
European Advisory Council, 35
Executive council, 41, 42
Exports, 81

Farming, 73
Fish, 58
Flag of Botswana, 49
Francistown, 22, 42, 51, 74, 76, 79, 86

Gaberone, Kgosi (chief), 67, 84
Gaborone (capital), 23, 30, 44, 45, 46, 51, 67, 79, 83, 84, 85
Gaborone Dam, 39
Geography, 11
Germans, 32, 35
Ghanzi (town), 79, 88
Ghanzi district, 34, 45, 88
Gold, 30, 34, 58, 75
Government, 50, 51

Health, 70, 71
Herero, 66
High Court of Botswana, 51
House of Chiefs, 44, 47, 49, 51
Houses, native, 68

Imports, 81
Income, per capita, 81
Independence, 49
Independence Party, 42, 45, 50
Industry, 74

Johannesburg, South Africa, 34, 78, 80
Joint Advisory Council, 40, 41

Kaa, 67
Kalahari Desert, 10, 12, 15, 16, 23-25, 27, 55, 58, 67, 88, 89
Kalaka, 67
Kanye, 75, 77, 79, 83
Kasane, 87
Kazungula, 79
Kgalagadi, 67
Kgalagadi district, 88
Kgotlas (councils), 35-7, 40
Kgwaketse district, 84
Kgwakgwe mine, 77
Khama I (chief), 66
Khama III (Khama the Great), 8, 9, 31, 32, 34, 36, 41, 64
Khama, Leapeetswa (chief), 64
Khama, Seretse, 36, 39-43, 46-50, 52, 63, 64, 76
Khama, Tshekedi (chief), 36, 39-41, 52
Kloisan language, 23
Koma, Kenneth, 47, 50
Kraal (enclosure), 69
Kumadow, Lake, 14
Kuruman, South Africa, 28
Kwena, 28

Labor, 80
Lakes, 12, 14
Land Boards, 70
Languages, 52, 62, 68
League of Nations, 35
Legislative Assembly, 44, 46, 49
Legislative council, 41, 42, 83
Lesotho, 23, 35, 53, 81
Letsholathebe (chief), 66
Limpopo River, 11, 14, 15, 31
Linchwe I (chief), 66
Linyanti (Chobe) River, 15
Literacy, 52
Livestock Improvement Center, 74, 75
Livingstone, David, 9, 11, 14, 28-30, 64, 86
Lobatse (town), 41, 44, 46, 51, 75, 79, 81, 83
London Conference, 1884, 32
London Missionary Society, 28, 30, 86
"Lost City of the Kalahari", 89
Lusaka, Zambia, 80

Mababe Depression, 14
Mafeking, 32, 34, 36, 45, 67, 83
Mahalapye, 86
Makarikari Salt Pans, 12, 14, 55, 58, 76, 86
Manufacturing, 75
Map of Botswana, 13
Map of Botswana councils, 51
Marico River, 11, 15
Masarwa (Bushmen), 67
Masilo, 28
Matabele, 28, 31, 65
Matante, P., 42, 50
Maun, 66, 78, 79, 87, 88
Mbukushu, 66
Meats, 75
Minerals, 58, 59, 75, 76
Mining, 20, 76, 80
Ministers, Cabinet, 51
Missionaries, 28, 30
Mochudi, 66
Moeng College, 37, 52
Moffat, Robert, 28, 29
Mokgosi, Kelemogile (chief), 67
Molepolole, 64, 79, 84, 86
Molopo River, 11, 32, 34
Monetary unit, 81
Montshiwa, Kebalepile (chief), 67
Moremi Wildlife Reserve, 78
Moshaweng, 67, 84
Motsete, Kgeleman T., 42
Mpho, Motsamai, 42, 50

Namibia (South West Africa), 11
Nata, 79, 87
National Archives, 84
National Assembly, 49, 50, 51, 84
National Front, 47, 50
National Library Service, 84
National Museum & Art Gallery, 84
Native Administration Proclamations, 36
Native Advisory Council, 35
Ndebele, 67
Newspapers, 80
Ngami, Lake, 12, 14, 74
Ngamiland, 12, 43, 65, 70, 71, 75, 78, 87
Ngobe River, 12
Ngwaketse, 28

Ngwato, 28
Nickel, 58, 76
Northern Rhodesia, 35, 46
North West district, 88
Nossob River, 11
Notwani River, 84

Okavango River, 12, 58, 74
Okavango Swamps, 12, 55, 58, 65, 87
Orange Free State, 30, 34
Orapa, 76, 79
Oxford University, 39

Palapye, 64, 79, 86
People's Party, 42, 46, 50
Pichos (public meetings), 37
Pickwe, 76
Pilane, M. (chief), 66
Pim Report, 35
Political parties, 42, 47
Pope Pius XII College, 53
Population density, 61
Population figures, 45, 61
Pretoria, South Africa, 31, 78
Pretoria Convention, 1881, 31, 32

Railroads, 8, 9, 34, 44, 78, 79
Rainfall, 10, 16, 17
Ramaquabane River, 11, 79
Ramathlabama, 79
Ramoutsa, 67
Rand (monetary unit), 81
Religion, 62, 63
Rhodes, Cecil, 8, 9, 32-34, 78
Rhodesia, 7, 11, 31, 35, 46, 47, 49, 50, 67, 75, 76, 78, 81, 87
Rivers, 11-15, 16
Roads, 28, 31, 32, 76, 79
Rural Training Centers, 73

Salt Pans, Makarikari, 12, 14, 55, 58, 76, 86
Schools, 20, 21-23, 37, 52, 53
Seasons, 16, 17
Sebele (chief), 8
Sebituane (chief), 29
Sechele, Neale (chief), 8, 30, 64, 65
Seepapito IV (chief), 65
Sekgoma (chief), 36
Selebi-Pickwe mines, 77
Sepopa, 74

Serondellas Camp, 87
Serowe, 64, 74, 76, 79, 83, 86
Setswana language, 52, 62
Shashi River, 11
Shushong, 19
South Africa, Republic of, 11, 20, 28, 32, 41, 45, 46, 47, 49, 75, 76, 80, 81
South Africa, Union of, 34, 35, 36, 39, 41
South African Customs Union, 81
South African War, 34
Southern Rhodesia, 35, 45
South West Africa, 11, 31, 32, 35, 39, 49, 66, 79, 88
Stanley, Henry M., 30

Swamps, Okavango, 12, 55, 58, 65, 87
Swaziland, 23, 34, 41, 81

Tanzania, 30
Tati Concession, 30, 34, 45, 49, 67, 79, 86
Tati River, 31
Tawana (chief), 65
Tlokwe, 67
Tourism, 76
Trade, 81
Transportation, 78-80
Transvaal, 7, 28, 30, 31, 32, 34, 64, 66
Treasuries, tribal, 36

Tsetse flies, 70, 71
Tshabong, 88
Tshane, 88
Tswana, 28

United Nations, 11, 39, 42, 45, 47, 76
United States of America, 50
University of Botswana, Lesotho, and Swaziland, 23, 53

Victoria, Queen, 7-9, 34
Victoria Falls, 11, 76
Villages, 68, 70

Warren, Charles, 32
Water resources, 59, 64
White population, 61
Williams, Ruth, 39
Willoughby, W. C., 8, 9
World War I, 35
World War II, 37

Xau, Lake, 12, 14, 74

Zambezi River, 11, 49, 76
Zambia, 11, 35, 46, 49, 50, 76, 79, 80, 86, 87
Zimbabwe (Rhodesia), 11
Zulu, 28

About the Author: Already the author of seventy-three books published by Childrens Press, Allan Carpenter is on his way again with the forty-two book "Enchantment of Africa" series. Except for a few years spent founding, editing, and publishing a teachers' magazine, Allan has worked as a free-lance writer of books and magazine articles. During his many years in publishing, he has perfected a highly organized approach to handling large volumes of material—after extensive traveling and having collected all possible materials, he systematically reviews and organizes everything. From his apartment high in the magnificent John Hancock Building, Allan recalls: "My collection and assimilation of materials on the states and countries began before the publication of my first book when I was twenty years old." When not writing or traveling, Allan also enjoys music—he has been the principal string bass player for the Chicago Business Men's Orchestra for twenty-five years.